PERSONA

Name:

Address:

Telephone: Email:

Employer:

Address:

Telephone: Email:

MEDICAL INFORMATION

Physician: Telephone:

Allergies:

Medications:

Blood Type:

Insurer:

IN CASE OF EMERGENCY, NOTIFY

Name:

Address:

Telephone: Relationship:

Our mission is to inspire the world with the life-changing message of the Bible.

Member of the
Evangelical Christian
Publishers Association

Printed in China.

2024

Gutsy Girl's
Creative Planner

BARBOUR
PUBLISHING

are You. . .

GUTSY?
COURAGEOUS?
FEARLESS?
BOLD? . . .

The truth is, when you have the Courage-Giver Himself by your side, you *can* live each day fear-free.

Every page of this creative planner will remind you of all the reasons it's possible (and important!) to be a gutsy girl of God. With each turn of the page, you'll encounter delightful, encouraging, devotional inspiration for your soul, plus monthly bulleted journaling pages. Each day of 2024, you'll be reminded that you *can* fully embrace the courageous life God intended you to live!

Gutsy girl, this is *your* year! Now go and live out God's amazing plan for your life!

> *Light, space, zest—that's GOD!*
> *So, with him on my side I'm fearless,*
> *afraid of no one and nothing.*
> PSALM 27:1 MSG

2024

JANUARY

S	M	T	W	T	F	S
	1	2	3	4	5	6
7	8	9	10	11	12	13
14	15	16	17	18	19	20
21	22	23	24	25	26	27
28	29	30	31			

FEBRUARY

S	M	T	W	T	F	S
				1	2	3
4	5	6	7	8	9	10
11	12	13	14	15	16	17
18	19	20	21	22	23	24
25	26	27	28	29		

MAY

S	M	T	W	T	F	S
			1	2	3	4
5	6	7	8	9	10	11
12	13	14	15	16	17	18
19	20	21	22	23	24	25
26	27	28	29	30	31	

JUNE

S	M	T	W	T	F	S
						1
2	3	4	5	6	7	8
9	10	11	12	13	14	15
16	17	18	19	20	21	22
23	24	25	26	27	28	29
30						

SEPTEMBER

S	M	T	W	T	F	S
1	2	3	4	5	6	7
8	9	10	11	12	13	14
15	16	17	18	19	20	21
22	23	24	25	26	27	28
29	30					

OCTOBER

S	M	T	W	T	F	S
		1	2	3	4	5
6	7	8	9	10	11	12
13	14	15	16	17	18	19
20	21	22	23	24	25	26
27	28	29	30	31		

Year at a Glance

MARCH

S	M	T	W	T	F	S
					1	2
3	4	5	6	7	8	9
10	11	12	13	14	15	16
17	18	19	20	21	22	23
24	25	26	27	28	29	30
31						

APRIL

S	M	T	W	T	F	S
	1	2	3	4	5	6
7	8	9	10	11	12	13
14	15	16	17	18	19	20
21	22	23	24	25	26	27
28	29	30				

JULY

S	M	T	W	T	F	S
	1	2	3	4	5	6
7	8	9	10	11	12	13
14	15	16	17	18	19	20
21	22	23	24	25	26	27
28	29	30	31			

AUGUST

S	M	T	W	T	F	S
				1	2	3
4	5	6	7	8	9	10
11	12	13	14	15	16	17
18	19	20	21	22	23	24
25	26	27	28	29	30	31

NOVEMBER

S	M	T	W	T	F	S
					1	2
3	4	5	6	7	8	9
10	11	12	13	14	15	16
17	18	19	20	21	22	23
24	25	26	27	28	29	30

DECEMBER

S	M	T	W	T	F	S
1	2	3	4	5	6	7
8	9	10	11	12	13	14
15	16	17	18	19	20	21
22	23	24	25	26	27	28
29	30	31				

August 2023

SUNDAY	MONDAY	TUESDAY	WEDNESDAY
30	31	1	2
6	7	8	9
13	14	15	16
20	21	22	23
27	28	29	30

THURSDAY	FRIDAY	SATURDAY
3	4	5
10	11	12
17	18	19
24	25	26
31	1	2

JULY

S	M	T	W	T	F	S
						1
2	3	4	5	6	7	8
9	10	11	12	13	14	15
16	17	18	19	20	21	22
23	24	25	26	27	28	29
30	31					

SEPTEMBER

S	M	T	W	T	F	S
					1	2
3	4	5	6	7	8	9
10	11	12	13	14	15	16
17	18	19	20	21	22	23
24	25	26	27	28	29	30

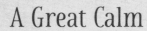

A Great Calm

Jesus holds power over every crisis you face. All the natural forces in and out of this world are under His control. Just as He can still a storm, Jesus can calm your mind, soothe your soul, relax your body, and charm your spirit. No matter how big or small your faith, Jesus will still reach out and save you.

Goals *for* This Month

He got up, rebuked the wind, and said to the sea, "Silence!
Be still!" The wind ceased, and there was a great calm. Then He
said to them, "Why are you fearful? Do you still have no faith?"
MARK 4:39–40 HCSB

July-August 2023

S	M	T	W	T	F	S
		1	2	3	4	5
6	7	8	9	10	11	12
13	14	15	16	17	18	19
20	21	22	23	24	25	26
27	28	29	30	31		

God never changes. Just as He cared and provided for Adam and Eve, He cares and provides for you. So put your fear, shame, and imperfections aside. Open yourself up to your Creator and His love.

to-do list

- [ ]
- [ ]
- [ ]
- [ ]
- [ ]
- [ ]
- [ ]
- [ ]
- [ ]
- [ ]
- [ ]
- [ ]
- [ ]
- [ ]
- [ ]
- [ ]
- [ ]

SUNDAY, July 30

MONDAY, July 31

TUESDAY, August 1

WEDNESDAY, August 2

THURSDAY, August 3

FRIDAY, August 4

SATURDAY, August 5

The Lord God made garments of skin for Adam and his wife and clothed them.
GENESIS 3:21 NIV

August 2023

S	M	T	W	T	F	S
		1	2	3	4	5
6	7	8	9	10	11	12
13	14	15	16	17	18	19
20	21	22	23	24	25	26
27	28	29	30	31		

The Father can erase your fears with a whisper. Jesus can still them with one motion. And the Holy Spirit can blow them away with one good exhale. Your Good Shepherd comes equipped with everything He needs to get you safely from one place to another.

to-do list

- [ ]
- [ ]
- [ ]
- [ ]
- [ ]
- [ ]
- [ ]
- [ ]
- [ ]
- [ ]
- [ ]
- [ ]
- [ ]
- [ ]
- [ ]
- [ ]
- [ ]
- [ ]
- [ ]

SUNDAY, August 6

MONDAY, August 7

TUESDAY, August 8

WEDNESDAY, August 9

....
....
....
....
....

THURSDAY, August 10

....
....
....
....
....

FRIDAY, August 11

....
....
....
....
....

SATURDAY, August 12

....
....
....
....
....

- ☐ ....
- ☐ ....
- ☐ ....
- ☐ ....
- ☐ ....
- ☐ ....
- ☐ ....
- ☐ ....
- ☐ ....
- ☐ ....
- ☐ ....
- ☐ ....
- ☐ ....

The Lord is my Shepherd [to feed, guide, and shield me], I shall not lack.... Yes, though I walk through the [deep, sunless] valley of the shadow of death, I will fear or dread no evil, for You are with me; Your rod [to protect] and Your staff [to guide], they comfort me.
PSALM 23:1, 4 AMPC

August 2023

S	M	T	W	T	F	S
		1	2	3	4	5
6	7	8	9	10	11	12
13	14	15	16	17	18	19
20	21	22	23	24	25	26
27	28	29	30	31		

God is not one to leave you stranded, to leave things unfinished. So, woman, trust God. Do not be afraid. He is committed to You, just as you are committed to Him.

to-do list

☐
☐
☐
☐
☐
☐
☐
☐
☐
☐
☐
☐
☐
☐
☐
☐
☐
☐
☐

SUNDAY, August 13

MONDAY, August 14

TUESDAY, August 15

WEDNESDAY, August 16

....

....

....

....

....

THURSDAY, August 17

....

....

....

....

....

FRIDAY, August 18

....

....

....

....

....

SATURDAY, August 19

....

....

....

....

....

to-do list

- ☐ ....
- ☐ ....
- ☐ ....
- ☐ ....
- ☐ ....
- ☐ ....
- ☐ ....
- ☐ ....
- ☐ ....
- ☐ ....
- ☐ ....
- ☐ ....
- ☐ ....
- ☐ ....

"When you pray, do not say the same thing over and over again making long prayers like the people who do not know God. They think they are heard because their prayers are long. Do not be like them. Your Father knows what you need before you ask Him."

MATTHEW 6:7–8 NLV

August 2023

S	M	T	W	T	F	S
		1	2	3	4	5
6	7	8	9	10	11	12
13	14	15	16	17	18	19
20	21	22	23	24	25	26
27	28	29	30	31		

Jesus has made it clear. He wants you to have the courage to live a faith-filled life in a nontraditional way. Jesus wants you to add power to your life by making spending time with Him your main goal.

to-do list

☐ ....
☐ ....
☐ ....
☐ ....
☐ ....
☐ ....
☐ ....
☐ ....
☐ ....
☐ ....
☐ ....
☐ ....
☐ ....
☐ ....
☐ ....
☐ ....
☐ ....
☐ ....

SUNDAY, August 20

....
....
....
....
....

MONDAY, August 21

....
....
....
....
....

TUESDAY, August 22

....
....
....
....
....

WEDNESDAY, August 23

....
....
....
....
....

THURSDAY, August 24

....
....
....
....
....

FRIDAY, August 25

....
....
....
....
....

SATURDAY, August 26

....
....
....
....
....

to-do list

☐ ....
☐ ....
☐ ....
☐ ....
☐ ....
☐ ....
☐ ....
☐ ....
☐ ....
☐ ....
☐ ....
☐ ....
☐ ....

*The Master said,
"Martha, dear Martha,
you're fussing far too
much and getting
yourself worked up over
nothing. One thing only
is essential, and Mary
has chosen it—it's the
main course, and won't
be taken from her."*
LUKE 10:41–42 MSG

August-September 2023

S	M	T	W	T	F	S
		1	2	3	4	5
6	7	8	9	10	11	12
13	14	15	16	17	18	19
20	21	22	23	24	25	26
27	28	29	30	31		

When you allow your faith to overcome your fear, when you focus on Christ alone, you find a new method of communication: you speak from your heart. Your actions and love speak louder than any words could.

to-do list

☐ ....
☐ ....
☐ ....
☐ ....
☐ ....
☐ ....
☐ ....
☐ ....
☐ ....
☐ ....
☐ ....
☐ ....
☐ ....
☐ ....
☐ ....
☐ ....
☐ ....
☐ ....

SUNDAY, August 27

MONDAY, August 28

TUESDAY, August 29

WEDNESDAY, August 30

THURSDAY, August 31

FRIDAY, September 1

SATURDAY, September 2

to-do list

☐
☐
☐
☐
☐
☐
☐
☐
☐
☐
☐
☐
☐
☐

When the disciples saw what was happening, they were furious. . . . [Jesus]. . .intervened. "Why are you giving this woman a hard time? She has just done something wonderfully significant for me. . . . What she has just done is going to be remembered and admired."

MATTHEW 26:8, 10, 13 MSG

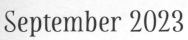

September 2023

SUNDAY	MONDAY	TUESDAY	WEDNESDAY
27	28	29	30
3	4 *Labor Day*	5	6
10	11	12	13
17	18	19	20
24	25	26	27

THURSDAY	FRIDAY	SATURDAY
1	1	2
7	8	9
14	15	16
21	22	23 *First Day of Autumn*
28	29	30

....
....
....
....
....
....
....
....
....
....
....
....
....

AUGUST

S	M	T	W	T	F	S
		1	2	3	4	5
6	7	8	9	10	11	12
13	14	15	16	17	18	19
20	21	22	23	24	25	26
27	28	29	30	31		

OCTOBER

S	M	T	W	T	F	S
1	2	3	4	5	6	7
8	9	10	11	12	13	14
15	16	17	18	19	20	21
22	23	24	25	26	27	28
29	30	31				

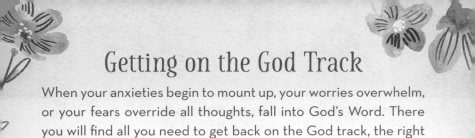

Getting on the God Track

When your anxieties begin to mount up, your worries overwhelm, or your fears override all thoughts, fall into God's Word. There you will find all you need to get back on the God track, the right path, the narrow yet better way.

Goals for This Month

In Him the whole fullness of Deity (the Godhead) continues to dwell in bodily form. . . . And you are in Him, made full and having come to fullness of life [in Christ you too are filled with the Godhead—Father, Son and Holy Spirit—and reach full spiritual stature]. And He is the Head of all rule and authority [of every angelic principality and power].

COLOSSIANS 2:9-10 AMPC

September 2023

S	M	T	W	T	F	S
					1	2
3	4	5	6	7	8	9
10	11	12	13	14	15	16
17	18	19	20	21	22	23
24	25	26	27	28	29	30

Be confident knowing that God wants you to be strong, unafraid, encouraged, and courageous. In fact, He commands you to: "Have not I commanded you? Be strong, vigorous, and very courageous. Be not afraid, neither be dismayed" (Joshua 1:9 AMPC).

to-do list

- [ ]
- [ ]
- [ ]
- [ ]
- [ ]
- [ ]
- [ ]
- [ ]
- [ ]
- [ ]
- [ ]
- [ ]
- [ ]
- [ ]
- [ ]
- [ ]
- [ ]
- [ ]

SUNDAY, September 3

MONDAY, September 4 *Labor Day*

TUESDAY, September 5

WEDNESDAY, September 6

....
....
....
....
....
....

THURSDAY, September 7

....
....
....
....
....
....

FRIDAY, September 8

....
....
....
....
....

SATURDAY, September 9

....
....
....
....
....

to-do list

☐ ....
☐ ....
☐ ....
☐ ....
☐ ....
☐ ....
☐ ....
☐ ....
☐ ....
☐ ....
☐ ....
☐ ....
☐ ....

This Book of the Law shall not depart out of your mouth, but you shall meditate on it day and night, that you may observe and do according to all that is written in it. For then you shall make your way prosperous...deal wisely and have good success.
JOSHUA 1:8 AMPC

September 2023

S	M	T	W	T	F	S
					1	2
3	4	5	6	7	8	9
10	11	12	13	14	15	16
17	18	19	20	21	22	23
24	25	26	27	28	29	30

Jesus wants you to boldly call out to Him and tell Him exactly what you need, taking a risk of faith. He is on your side! He, the ultimate authority in heaven and earth, sticks up for you.

to-do list

- [ ] ....
- [ ] ....
- [ ] ....
- [ ] ....
- [ ] ....
- [ ] ....
- [ ] ....
- [ ] ....
- [ ] ....
- [ ] ....
- [ ] ....
- [ ] ....
- [ ] ....
- [ ] ....
- [ ] ....
- [ ] ....
- [ ] ....
- [ ] ....

SUNDAY, September 10

....

....

....

....

....

MONDAY, September 11

....

....

....

....

....

TUESDAY, September 12

....

....

....

....

....

WEDNESDAY, September 13

....
....
....
....
....

THURSDAY, September 14

....
....
....
....
....

FRIDAY, September 15

....
....
....
....
....

SATURDAY, September 16

....
....
....
....
....

to-do list

- [ ] ....
- [ ] ....
- [ ] ....
- [ ] ....
- [ ] ....
- [ ] ....
- [ ] ....
- [ ] ....
- [ ] ....
- [ ] ....
- [ ] ....
- [ ] ....
- [ ] ....
- [ ] ....
- [ ] ....
- [ ] ....
- [ ] ....
- [ ] ....

*Faith comes from
hearing, and hearing
through the word
of Christ.*
ROMANS 10:17 ESV

September 2023

S	M	T	W	T	F	S
					1	2
3	4	5	6	7	8	9
10	11	12	13	14	15	16
17	18	19	20	21	22	23
24	25	26	27	28	29	30

Even though you may be known only as someone's mother, wife, or daughter, don't despair. God sees you, knows your potential, and has a plan for you alone. Simply remain content, confident, and unshakable as you wait, hope, and expect His direction.

to-do list

- [ ]
- [ ]
- [ ]
- [ ]
- [ ]
- [ ]
- [ ]
- [ ]
- [ ]
- [ ]
- [ ]
- [ ]
- [ ]
- [ ]
- [ ]
- [ ]
- [ ]
- [ ]

SUNDAY, September 17

MONDAY, September 18

TUESDAY, September 19

WEDNESDAY, September 20

....
....
....
....
....

THURSDAY, September 21

....
....
....
....
....

FRIDAY, September 22

....
....
....
....
....

SATURDAY, September 23 *First Day of Autumn*

....
....
....
....
....

to-do list

- ☐ ....
- ☐ ....
- ☐ ....
- ☐ ....
- ☐ ....
- ☐ ....
- ☐ ....
- ☐ ....
- ☐ ....
- ☐ ....
- ☐ ....
- ☐ ....
- ☐ ....
- ☐ ....

The woman came and told her husband, "A man of God came to me, and his appearance was like the appearance of the angel of God, very awesome. I did not ask him where he was from, and he did not tell me his name, but he said to me, 'Behold, you shall conceive and bear a son.'"
JUDGES 13:6-7 ESV

September 2023

S	M	T	W	T	F	S
					1	2
3	4	5	6	7	8	9
10	11	12	13	14	15	16
17	18	19	20	21	22	23
24	25	26	27	28	29	30

When God is with you, *anything* can happen. With Him by your side, you can achieve the seemingly unachievable. By faithfully following His directives, you can overcome any obstacle. With trust in Him, you can be courageous and experience the impossible.

to-do list

- [ ]
- [ ]
- [ ]
- [ ]
- [ ]
- [ ]
- [ ]
- [ ]
- [ ]
- [ ]
- [ ]
- [ ]
- [ ]
- [ ]
- [ ]
- [ ]
- [ ]
- [ ]

SUNDAY, September 24

MONDAY, September 25

TUESDAY, September 26

WEDNESDAY, September 27

- [ ]
- [ ]
- [ ]
- [ ]
- [ ]
- [ ]
- [ ]
- [ ]
- [ ]
- [ ]
- [ ]
- [ ]
- [ ]

THURSDAY, September 28

FRIDAY, September 29

"Today I will begin to exalt you in the sight of all Israel, so they will know that I will be with you just as I was with Moses. Command the priests carrying the ark of the covenant: When you reach the edge of the waters, stand in the Jordan."

JOSHUA 3:7–8 HCSB

SATURDAY, September 30

October 2023

SUNDAY	MONDAY	TUESDAY	WEDNESDAY
1	2	3	4
8	9 *Columbus Day*	10	11
15	16	17	18
22	23	24	25
29	30	31 *Halloween*	1

THURSDAY	FRIDAY	SATURDAY
5	6	7
12	13	14
19	20	21
26	27	28
2	3	4

notes

....
....
....
....
....
....
....
....
....
....
....

SEPTEMBER

S	M	T	W	T	F	S
					1	2
3	4	5	6	7	8	9
10	11	12	13	14	15	16
17	18	19	20	21	22	23
24	25	26	27	28	29	30

NOVEMBER

S	M	T	W	T	F	S
			1	2	3	4
5	6	7	8	9	10	11
12	13	14	15	16	17	18
19	20	21	22	23	24	25
26	27	28	29	30		

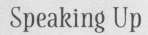

Speaking Up

When it comes time for you to speak up—for God, for the help-less, for the voiceless, for yourself—leave fear behind. Don't worry about how you will be judged, what you will say, or how people will receive your words. Instead, take some time in the moment to pray, asking God what He would have you say—or not say. Believe His promise, trusting His Spirit to fill your heart, head, and mouth with His words.

Goals *for* This Month

*Speak up for those who have no voice, for the justice
of all who are dispossessed. Speak up. . .and defend
the cause of the oppressed and needy.*
PROVERBS 31:8-9 HCSB

October 2023

S	M	T	W	T	F	S
1	2	3	4	5	6	7
8	9	10	11	12	13	14
15	16	17	18	19	20	21
22	23	24	25	26	27	28
29	30	31				

Take heart. God has thoughts and plans for you—plans for your good, ones that give you hope for your future (see Jeremiah 29:11). And He will do so much more than you ever "ask or think through His power working" in you (Ephesians 3:20 NLV).

to-do list

- [ ]
- [ ]
- [ ]
- [ ]
- [ ]
- [ ]
- [ ]
- [ ]
- [ ]
- [ ]
- [ ]
- [ ]
- [ ]
- [ ]
- [ ]
- [ ]
- [ ]
- [ ]
- [ ]

SUNDAY, October 1

MONDAY, October 2

TUESDAY, October 3

WEDNESDAY, October 4

THURSDAY, October 5

FRIDAY, October 6

Without faith it is impossible to please and be satisfactory to Him. For whoever would come near to God must [necessarily] believe that God exists and that He is the rewarder of those who earnestly and diligently seek Him [out].
HEBREWS 11:6 AMPC

SATURDAY, October 7

October 2023

S	M	T	W	T	F	S
1	2	3	4	5	6	7
8	9	10	11	12	13	14
15	16	17	18	19	20	21
22	23	24	25	26	27	28
29	30	31				

Gather up your courage and step out of your comfort zone. Consider what talents you may have been neglecting or what gifts, opportunities, or resources you have put on the back burner. Be faithful with what you have been given, and God will give you more.

to-do list

- [ ] ....
- [ ] ....
- [ ] ....
- [ ] ....
- [ ] ....
- [ ] ....
- [ ] ....
- [ ] ....
- [ ] ....
- [ ] ....
- [ ] ....
- [ ] ....
- [ ] ....
- [ ] ....
- [ ] ....
- [ ] ....
- [ ] ....
- [ ] ....

SUNDAY, October 8

MONDAY, October 9   *Columbus Day*

TUESDAY, October 10

WEDNESDAY, October 11

....
....
....
....
....

THURSDAY, October 12

....
....
....
....
....

FRIDAY, October 13

....
....
....
....
....

SATURDAY, October 14

....
....
....
....
....

to-do list

☐ ....
☐ ....
☐ ....
☐ ....
☐ ....
☐ ....
☐ ....
☐ ....
☐ ....
☐ ....
☐ ....
☐ ....
☐ ....
☐ ....
☐ ....
☐ ....
☐ ....
☐ ....

"Well done, good and faithful slave! You were faithful over a few things; I will put you in charge of many things. Share your master's joy!"
MATTHEW 25:21 HCSB

October 2023

S	M	T	W	T	F	S
1	2	3	4	5	6	7
8	9	10	11	12	13	14
15	16	17	18	19	20	21
22	23	24	25	26	27	28
29	30	31				

Remember that, although the material world may pass through your fingers, God and His Word will never fade away. God and His love are eternally yours. He will never leave you.

to-do list

- ☐
- ☐
- ☐
- ☐
- ☐
- ☐
- ☐
- ☐
- ☐
- ☐
- ☐
- ☐
- ☐
- ☐
- ☐
- ☐
- ☐
- ☐
- ☐

SUNDAY, October 15

MONDAY, October 16

TUESDAY, October 17

WEDNESDAY, October 18

....
....
....
....
....

THURSDAY, October 19

....
....
....
....
....

FRIDAY, October 20

....
....
....
....
....

SATURDAY, October 21

....
....
....
....
....

to-do list

☐ ....
☐ ....
☐ ....
☐ ....
☐ ....
☐ ....
☐ ....
☐ ....
☐ ....
☐ ....
☐ ....

"You are going to hear of wars and rumors of wars. See that you are not alarmed, because these things must take place, but the end is not yet. For nation will rise up against nation, and kingdom against kingdom. There will be famines and earthquakes in various places.... Heaven and earth will pass away, but My words will never pass away."

MATTHEW 24:6–7, 35 HCSB

October 2023

S	M	T	W	T	F	S
1	2	3	4	5	6	7
8	9	10	11	12	13	14
15	16	17	18	19	20	21
22	23	24	25	26	27	28
29	30	31				

God, your heavenly protector, will cover you with His wings. Because of His presence, because He's your refuge, you need not be afraid of anything, for nothing untoward can touch you.

to-do list

☐ ....
☐ ....
☐ ....
☐ ....
☐ ....
☐ ....
☐ ....
☐ ....
☐ ....
☐ ....
☐ ....
☐ ....
☐ ....
☐ ....
☐ ....
☐ ....
☐ ....
☐ ....
☐ ....

SUNDAY, October 22

MONDAY, October 23

TUESDAY, October 24

WEDNESDAY, October 25

THURSDAY, October 26

FRIDAY, October 27

SATURDAY, October 28

☐ ....
☐ ....
☐ ....
☐ ....
☐ ....
☐ ....
☐ ....
☐ ....
☐ ....
☐ ....
☐ ....
☐ ....
☐ ....

He who dwells in the secret place of the Most High shall remain stable and fixed under the shadow of the Almighty [Whose power no foe can withstand]. I will say of the Lord, He is my Refuge and my Fortress, my God; on Him I lean and rely, and in Him I [confidently] trust! . . . You shall not be afraid.
PSALM 91:1-2, 5 AMPC

November 2023

SUNDAY	MONDAY	TUESDAY	WEDNESDAY
29	30	31	1
5 *Daylight Saving Time Ends*	6	7 *Election Day*	8
12	13	14	15
19	20	21	22
26	27	28	29

THURSDAY	FRIDAY	SATURDAY
2	3	4
9	10	11
	Veterans Day	
16	17	18
23	24	25
Thanksgiving Day		
30	1	2

notes

....
....
....
....
....
....
....
....
....
....
....
....
....

OCTOBER

S	M	T	W	T	F	S
1	2	3	4	5	6	7
8	9	10	11	12	13	14
15	16	17	18	19	20	21
22	23	24	25	26	27	28
29	30	31				

DECEMBER

S	M	T	W	T	F	S
					1	2
3	4	5	6	7	8	9
10	11	12	13	14	15	16
17	18	19	20	21	22	23
24	25	26	27	28	29	30
31						

The Road Home

You may have times when you make mistakes and feel a bit bitter that life has treated you unfairly. But even during those times, may you have the courage to continue to be a loving example for younger women trying to find their own way home in the Lord.

Goals for This Month

Go, return each of you to her mother's house. May the Lord deal kindly with you, as you have dealt with the dead and with me. The Lord grant that you may find a home and rest, each in the house of her husband!

RUTH 1:8-9 AMPC

October–November 2023

S	M	T	W	T	F	S
				1	2	3	4
5	6	7	8	9	10	11
12	13	14	15	16	17	18
19	20	21	22	23	24	25
26	27	28	29	30		

Take courage. Throw away the unnecessaries, the distractions, the entanglements. Then walk face-first and at full speed to Jesus, keeping your eyes of hope and faith on Him.

to-do list

- [ ]
- [ ]
- [ ]
- [ ]
- [ ]
- [ ]
- [ ]
- [ ]
- [ ]
- [ ]
- [ ]
- [ ]
- [ ]
- [ ]
- [ ]
- [ ]
- [ ]
- [ ]

SUNDAY, October 29

MONDAY, October 30

TUESDAY, October 31   *Halloween*

WEDNESDAY, November 1

THURSDAY, November 2

FRIDAY, November 3

SATURDAY, November 4

to-do list

☐ ....

☐ ....

☐ ....

☐ ....

☐ ....

☐ ....

☐ ....

☐ ....

☐ ....

☐ ....

Let us. . .throw aside every encumbrance (unnecessary weight) and that sin which so readily (deftly and cleverly) clings to and entangles us, and let us run with patient endurance. . .the appointed course of the race that is set before us, looking away [from all that will distract] to Jesus, Who is the Leader and the Source of our faith.
HEBREWS 12:1–2 AMPC

November 2023

S	M	T	W	T	F	S
			1	2	3	4
5	6	7	8	9	10	11
12	13	14	15	16	17	18
19	20	21	22	23	24	25
26	27	28	29	30		

Those who put their roots deep into the foundation of faith, hope, and love that the Lord provides us will have endurance and perseverance. Even when hard times make it difficult to push through, their relationship with the Lord will help them be strong and confident.

to-do list

- ☐ ....
- ☐ ....
- ☐ ....
- ☐ ....
- ☐ ....
- ☐ ....
- ☐ ....
- ☐ ....
- ☐ ....
- ☐ ....
- ☐ ....
- ☐ ....
- ☐ ....
- ☐ ....
- ☐ ....
- ☐ ....
- ☐ ....
- ☐ ....
- ☐ ....

SUNDAY, November 5   *Daylight Saving Time Ends*

....
....
....
....
....

MONDAY, November 6

....
....
....
....
....

TUESDAY, November 7   *Election Day*

....
....
....
....
....

WEDNESDAY, November 8

THURSDAY, November 9

FRIDAY, November 10

SATURDAY, November 11   *Veterans Day*

☐
☐
☐
☐
☐
☐
☐
☐
☐
☐
☐
☐
☐
☐
☐
☐
☐
☐
☐

"But blessed is the one who trusts in the LORD, whose confidence is in him."
JEREMIAH 17:7 NIV

November 2023

S	M	T	W	T	F	S
			1	2	3	4
5	6	7	8	9	10	11
12	13	14	15	16	17	18
19	20	21	22	23	24	25
26	27	28	29	30		

Because you are a believer, a daughter of God the King, you will lack for nothing. Ever. So do not fear. Jesus has His eyes on you. He knows exactly what you need and will provide it exactly when you need it. Until then, continue to have courage and faith.

to-do list

- [ ]
- [ ]
- [ ]
- [ ]
- [ ]
- [ ]
- [ ]
- [ ]
- [ ]
- [ ]
- [ ]
- [ ]
- [ ]
- [ ]
- [ ]
- [ ]
- [ ]
- [ ]
- [ ]
- [ ]

SUNDAY, November 12

MONDAY, November 13

TUESDAY, November 14

WEDNESDAY, November 15

THURSDAY, November 16

FRIDAY, November 17

SATURDAY, November 18

to-do list

☐
☐
☐
☐
☐
☐
☐
☐
☐
☐
☐
☐
☐
☐

So, my very dear friends, don't get thrown off course. Every desirable and beneficial gift comes out of heaven. The gifts are rivers of light cascading down from the Father of Light. There is nothing deceitful in God, nothing two-faced, nothing fickle.

JAMES 1:16–17 MSG

November 2023

S	M	T	W	T	F	S
			1	2	3	4
5	6	7	8	9	10	11
12	13	14	15	16	17	18
19	20	21	22	23	24	25
26	27	28	29	30		

Perhaps there is something you need but have yet to ask for. If so, take some time to consider what you have and evaluate what you need. Then gather up your courage and ask God, knowing that if you do so, you will receive (see Matthew 7:7).

to-do list

- [ ]
- [ ]
- [ ]
- [ ]
- [ ]
- [ ]
- [ ]
- [ ]
- [ ]
- [ ]
- [ ]
- [ ]
- [ ]
- [ ]
- [ ]
- [ ]
- [ ]
- [ ]

SUNDAY, November 19

MONDAY, November 20

TUESDAY, November 21

WEDNESDAY, November 22

....
....
....
....
....

THURSDAY, November 23   *Thanksgiving Day*

....
....
....
....
....

FRIDAY, November 24

....
....
....
....
....

SATURDAY, November 25

....
....
....
....
....

to-do list

☐ ....
☐ ....
☐ ....
☐ ....
☐ ....
☐ ....
☐ ....
☐ ....
☐ ....
☐ ....
☐ ....
☐ ....

*When Achsah came
to Othniel, she got
his consent to ask her
father for a field. Then
she returned to Caleb
and when she lighted
off her donkey, Caleb
said, What do you wish?
Achsah answered, Give
me a present. Since
you have set me in the
[dry] Negeb, give me
also springs of water.*
JOSHUA 15:18–19 AMPC

November–December 2023

S	M	T	W	T	F	S
			1	2	3	4
5	6	7	8	9	10	11
12	13	14	15	16	17	18
19	20	21	22	23	24	25
26	27	28	29	30		

No matter where you are in your walk with God, no matter how you approach Jesus, brazenly or beggarly, He will not only heal you but, upon your approach, also put you at ease with words of encouragement and affection.

to-do list

- [ ] ....
- [ ] ....
- [ ] ....
- [ ] ....
- [ ] ....
- [ ] ....
- [ ] ....
- [ ] ....
- [ ] ....
- [ ] ....
- [ ] ....
- [ ] ....
- [ ] ....
- [ ] ....
- [ ] ....
- [ ] ....
- [ ] ....
- [ ] ....
- [ ] ....

SUNDAY, November 26

MONDAY, November 27

TUESDAY, November 28

WEDNESDAY, November 29

THURSDAY, November 30

FRIDAY, December 1

SATURDAY, December 2

to-do list

☐
☐
☐
☐
☐
☐
☐
☐
☐
☐
☐
☐
☐
☐
☐

Some men brought to [Jesus] a paralytic lying on a mat. Seeing their faith, Jesus told the paralytic, "Have courage, son, your sins are forgiven.... Get up, pick up your mat, and go home." And he got up and went home.
MATTHEW 9:2, 6–7 HCSB

December 2023

SUNDAY	MONDAY	TUESDAY	WEDNESDAY
26	27	28	29
3	4	5	6
10	11	12	13
17	18	19	20
24 *Christmas Eve* / *New Year's Eve* 31	25 *Christmas Day*	26	27

THURSDAY	FRIDAY	SATURDAY
30	1	2
7 *Hanukkah Begins at Sundown*	8	9
14	15	16
21 *First Day of Winter*	22	23
28	29	30

notes

....
....
....
....
....
....
....
....
....
....
....
....

NOVEMBER

S	M	T	W	T	F	S
			1	2	3	4
5	6	7	8	9	10	11
12	13	14	15	16	17	18
19	20	21	22	23	24	25
26	27	28	29	30		

JANUARY

S	M	T	W	T	F	S
	1	2	3	4	5	6
7	8	9	10	11	12	13
14	15	16	17	18	19	20
21	22	23	24	25	26	27
28	29	30	31			

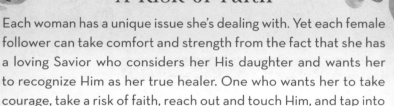

A Risk of Faith

Each woman has a unique issue she's dealing with. Yet each female follower can take comfort and strength from the fact that she has a loving Savior who considers her His daughter and wants her to recognize Him as her true healer. One who wants her to take courage, take a risk of faith, reach out and touch Him, and tap into His power—and to share her story of transformation.

Goals *for* This Month

[The woman who had been sick for twelve years with a flow of blood] told Jesus in front of all the people why she had touched Him. She told how she was healed at once. Jesus said to her, "Daughter, your faith has healed you. Go in peace."
LUKE 8:47–48 NLV

December 2023

S	M	T	W	T	F	S
					1	2
3	4	5	6	7	8	9
10	11	12	13	14	15	16
17	18	19	20	21	22	23
24	25	26	27	28	29	30
31						

Close your eyes, lean back, and hear God speaking His Word in that voice reserved just for you. Then imagine God's Son touching you, speaking to your heart of hearts, saying, "Get up, and do not be afraid."

to-do list

- ☐ ....
- ☐ ....
- ☐ ....
- ☐ ....
- ☐ ....
- ☐ ....
- ☐ ....
- ☐ ....
- ☐ ....
- ☐ ....
- ☐ ....
- ☐ ....
- ☐ ....
- ☐ ....
- ☐ ....
- ☐ ....
- ☐ ....

SUNDAY, December 3

MONDAY, December 4

TUESDAY, December 5

WEDNESDAY, December 6

THURSDAY, December 7 *Hanukkah Begins at Sundown*

FRIDAY, December 8

SATURDAY, December 9

to-do list

☐
☐
☐
☐
☐
☐
☐
☐
☐
☐
☐
☐
☐
☐
☐
☐

*Be not afraid. . .for
I am with you. . . . I
am alert and active,
watching over My word
to perform it. . . . Jesus
came and touched
them and said, Get up,
and do not be afraid.*
JEREMIAH 1:8, 12;
MATTHEW 17:7 AMPC

December 2023

S	M	T	W	T	F	S
					1	2
3	4	5	6	7	8	9
10	11	12	13	14	15	16
17	18	19	20	21	22	23
24	25	26	27	28	29	30
31						

Know that wherever you go, whatever the circumstances, time, or place, God is with you. He hears your prayers. He knows your fears. He is with you, helping you, guiding you. You only need to trust that He's doing so—right now.

to-do list

- [ ]
- [ ]
- [ ]
- [ ]
- [ ]
- [ ]
- [ ]
- [ ]
- [ ]
- [ ]
- [ ]
- [ ]
- [ ]
- [ ]
- [ ]
- [ ]
- [ ]
- [ ]

SUNDAY, December 10

MONDAY, December 11

TUESDAY, December 12

WEDNESDAY, December 13

THURSDAY, December 14

FRIDAY, December 15

SATURDAY, December 16

to-do list

- [ ] ....
- [ ] ....
- [ ] ....
- [ ] ....
- [ ] ....
- [ ] ....
- [ ] ....
- [ ] ....
- [ ] ....
- [ ] ....
- [ ] ....
- [ ] ....
- [ ] ....

Hide not Your face from me in the day when I am in distress! Incline Your ear to me; in the day when I call, answer me speedily.... Have pity and compassion.... He will regard the plea of the destitute and will not despise their prayer.
PSALM 102:2, 13, 17 AMPC

December 2023

S	M	T	W	T	F	S
					1	2
3	4	5	6	7	8	9
10	11	12	13	14	15	16
17	18	19	20	21	22	23
24	25	26	27	28	29	30
31						

When you're feeling helpless, hopeless, and hapless, Jesus has five words He wants you to remember, to repeat, to write on your heart and mind: "Don't be afraid. Only believe."

to-do list

- [ ]
- [ ]
- [ ]
- [ ]
- [ ]
- [ ]
- [ ]
- [ ]
- [ ]
- [ ]
- [ ]
- [ ]
- [ ]
- [ ]
- [ ]
- [ ]
- [ ]
- [ ]

SUNDAY, December 17

MONDAY, December 18

TUESDAY, December 19

WEDNESDAY, December 20

....
....
....
....
....

THURSDAY, December 21   *First Day of Winter*

....
....
....
....
....

FRIDAY, December 22

....
....
....
....
....

SATURDAY, December 23

....
....
....
....
....

- [ ] ....
- [ ] ....
- [ ] ....
- [ ] ....
- [ ] ....
- [ ] ....
- [ ] ....
- [ ] ....
- [ ] ....
- [ ] ....
- [ ] ....
- [ ] ....
- [ ] ....

People came from the synagogue leader's house and said, "Your daughter is dead. Why bother the Teacher anymore?" But when Jesus overheard what was said, He told the synagogue leader, "Don't be afraid. Only believe."
MARK 5:35–36 HCSB

December 2023

S	M	T	W	T	F	S
					1	2
3	4	5	6	7	8	9
10	11	12	13	14	15	16
17	18	19	20	21	22	23
24	25	26	27	28	29	30
31						

In your quest to do as God wills, trust God to show you the way. Then rise up quickly when He says the time is right, encouraging those you're leading. But most of all, remember that God is going before you. He is clearing your path to victory.

to-do list

- [ ] ....
- [ ] ....
- [ ] ....
- [ ] ....
- [ ] ....
- [ ] ....
- [ ] ....
- [ ] ....
- [ ] ....
- [ ] ....
- [ ] ....
- [ ] ....
- [ ] ....
- [ ] ....
- [ ] ....
- [ ] ....
- [ ] ....
- [ ] ....

SUNDAY, December 24　　　*Christmas Eve*

....

....

....

....

....

MONDAY, December 25　　　*Christmas Day*

....

....

....

....

....

TUESDAY, December 26

....

....

....

....

....

WEDNESDAY, December 27

....
....
....
....
....

THURSDAY, December 28

....
....
....
....
....

FRIDAY, December 29

....
....
....
....
....

SATURDAY, December 30

....
....
....
....
....

to-do list

- ☐ ....
- ☐ ....
- ☐ ....
- ☐ ....
- ☐ ....
- ☐ ....
- ☐ ....
- ☐ ....
- ☐ ....
- ☐ ....
- ☐ ....
- ☐ ....
- ☐ ....
- ☐ ....
- ☐ ....

And Deborah arose and went with Barak to Kedesh. . . . The villages were unoccupied and rulers ceased in Israel until you arose—you, Deborah, arose—a mother in Israel.
JUDGES 4:9; 5:7 AMPC

January 2024

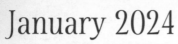

SUNDAY	MONDAY	TUESDAY	WEDNESDAY
31	1 New Year's Day	2	3
7	8	9	10
14	15 Martin Luther King Jr. Day	16	17
21	22	23	24
28	29	30	31

THURSDAY	FRIDAY	SATURDAY
4	5	6
11	12	13
18	19	20
25	26	27
1	2	3

notes

....
....
....
....
....
....
....
....
....
....
....
....
....

DECEMBER

S	M	T	W	T	F	S
					1	2
3	4	5	6	7	8	9
10	11	12	13	14	15	16
17	18	19	20	21	22	23
24	25	26	27	28	29	30
31						

FEBRUARY

S	M	T	W	T	F	S
				1	2	3
4	5	6	7	8	9	10
11	12	13	14	15	16	17
18	19	20	21	22	23	24
25	26	27	28	29		

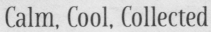

Calm, Cool, Collected

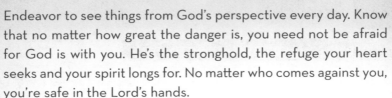

Endeavor to see things from God's perspective every day. Know that no matter how great the danger is, you need not be afraid for God is with you. He's the stronghold, the refuge your heart seeks and your spirit longs for. No matter who comes against you, you're safe in the Lord's hands.

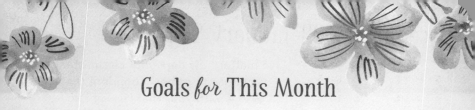

Goals *for* This Month

*The Lord is my light and the One Who saves me. Whom
should I fear? The Lord is the strength of my life. Of whom
should I be afraid? . . . Even if an army gathers against me,
my heart will not be afraid. . . . I will be sure of You.*

PSALM 27:1, 3 NLV

December 2023-January 2024

S	M	T	W	T	F	S
					1	2	3	4	5	6

S	M	T	W	T	F	S
					1	2
3	4	5	6
7	8	9	10	11	12	13
14	15	16	17	18	19	20
21	22	23	24	25	26	27
28	29	30	31

No matter how dark your circumstances, choose to remain confident that God is with you. That His light, love, and compassion are streaming down upon you. That He will rescue you with His might and miracles.

to-do list

- [ ]
- [ ]
- [ ]
- [ ]
- [ ]
- [ ]
- [ ]
- [ ]
- [ ]
- [ ]
- [ ]
- [ ]
- [ ]
- [ ]
- [ ]
- [ ]
- [ ]
- [ ]

SUNDAY, December 31 *New Year's Eve*

MONDAY, January 1 *New Year's Day*

TUESDAY, January 2

WEDNESDAY, January 3

THURSDAY, January 4

FRIDAY, January 5

SATURDAY, January 6

to-do list

☐

☐

☐

☐

☐

☐

☐

☐

☐

☐

☐

☐

☐

*I will be to you a God;
and you shall know that
it is I, the Lord your God,
Who brings you out from
under the burdens of
the Egyptians.... Moses
told this to the Israelites,
but they refused to
listen to Moses because
of their impatience
and anguish of spirit
and...cruel bondage.*

EXODUS 6:7, 9 AMPC

January 2024

S	M	T	W	T	F	S
	1	2	3	4	5	6
7	8	9	10	11	12	13
14	15	16	17	18	19	20
21	22	23	24	25	26	27
28	29	30	31			

No matter what storms you're trying to get through, you can remain unafraid. Remember that God is right here with you. He has climbed into your boat. He's telling you how to navigate through rough waters. He's calming you within and without.

to-do list

- [ ]
- [ ]
- [ ]
- [ ]
- [ ]
- [ ]
- [ ]
- [ ]
- [ ]
- [ ]
- [ ]
- [ ]
- [ ]
- [ ]
- [ ]
- [ ]
- [ ]
- [ ]
- [ ]

SUNDAY, January 7

MONDAY, January 8

TUESDAY, January 9

WEDNESDAY, January 10

- [ ] ....
- [ ] ....
- [ ] ....
- [ ] ....
- [ ] ....
- [ ] ....

THURSDAY, January 11

- [ ] ....
- [ ] ....
- [ ] ....
- [ ] ....
- [ ] ....
- [ ] ....

FRIDAY, January 12

- [ ] ....
- [ ] ....
- [ ] ....
- [ ] ....
- [ ] ....

SATURDAY, January 13

Immediately [Jesus] spoke with [His disciples] and said, "Have courage! It is I. Don't be afraid."
MARK 6:50 HCSB

January 2024

S	M	T	W	T	F	S
	1	2	3	4	5	6
7	8	9	10	11	12	13
14	15	16	17	18	19	20
21	22	23	24	25	26	27
28	29	30	31			

Remember that all your power and ability to be courageous, to step out of your comfort zone and do what circumstances require, are due solely to God's presence in your life. Count on Him alone. And as you do, God will then be able to count on you.

to-do list

- [ ] ....
- [ ] ....
- [ ] ....
- [ ] ....
- [ ] ....
- [ ] ....
- [ ] ....
- [ ] ....
- [ ] ....
- [ ] ....
- [ ] ....
- [ ] ....
- [ ] ....
- [ ] ....
- [ ] ....
- [ ] ....
- [ ] ....
- [ ] ....

SUNDAY, January 14

MONDAY, January 15   *Martin Luther King Jr. Day*

TUESDAY, January 16

WEDNESDAY, January 17

THURSDAY, January 18

FRIDAY, January 19

SATURDAY, January 20

to-do list

- [ ]
- [ ]
- [ ]
- [ ]
- [ ]
- [ ]
- [ ]
- [ ]
- [ ]
- [ ]
- [ ]
- [ ]
- [ ]

"Do whatever your circumstances require because God is with you." . . . Who is qualified (fit and sufficient) for these things? . . . Not that we are fit (qualified and sufficient in ability) of ourselves. . .but our power and ability and sufficiency are from God.

1 SAMUEL 10:7 HCSB;
2 CORINTHIANS 2:16;
3:5 AMPC

January 2024

S	M	T	W	T	F	S
	1	2	3	4	5	6
7	8	9	10	11	12	13
14	15	16	17	18	19	20
21	22	23	24	25	26	27
28	29	30	31			

It is Jesus' light that shines in our lives today. It is His light that draws us to Him. It is His light that we stand in to confess our sins and be forgiven. It is His light that sets us free.

to-do list

- ☐ ....
- ☐ ....
- ☐ ....
- ☐ ....
- ☐ ....
- ☐ ....
- ☐ ....
- ☐ ....
- ☐ ....
- ☐ ....
- ☐ ....
- ☐ ....
- ☐ ....
- ☐ ....
- ☐ ....
- ☐ ....
- ☐ ....
- ☐ ....

SUNDAY, January 21

....
....
....
....
....

MONDAY, January 22

....
....
....
....
....

TUESDAY, January 23

....
....
....
....
....

WEDNESDAY, January 24

THURSDAY, January 25

FRIDAY, January 26

SATURDAY, January 27

to-do list

- [ ]
- [ ]
- [ ]
- [ ]
- [ ]
- [ ]
- [ ]
- [ ]
- [ ]
- [ ]
- [ ]
- [ ]
- [ ]
- [ ]
- [ ]
- [ ]
- [ ]
- [ ]
- [ ]

"I am the light of the world. Whoever follows me will never walk in darkness, but will have the light of life."
JOHN 8:12 NIV

February 2024

SUNDAY	MONDAY	TUESDAY	WEDNESDAY
28	29	30	31
4	5	6	7
11	12	13	14 *Ash Wednesday* *Valentine's Day*
18	19 *Presidents' Day*	20	21
25	26	27	28

THURSDAY	FRIDAY	SATURDAY
1	2	3
8	9	10
15	16	17
22	23	24
29 *Leap Day*	1	2

....
....
....
....
....
....
....
....
....
....
....
....

JANUARY

S	M	T	W	T	F	S
		1	2	3	4	5	6
7	8	9	10	11	12	13
14	15	16	17	18	19	20
21	22	23	24	25	26	27
28	29	30	31			

MARCH

S	M	T	W	T	F	S
					1	2
3	4	5	6	7	8	9
10	11	12	13	14	15	16
17	18	19	20	21	22	23
24	25	26	27	28	29	30
31						

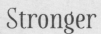

Stronger

Thankfully we have a source we can go to when we become so tired that we find it hard to stand on truth, to act in love, and to extend grace. We can ask for help and wisdom from the one who has a limitless supply of both. We can ask for refreshment and innovation from the Creator God who formed this world from end to end. When we are at our weakest, He can make us stronger. When we are without hope, He can renew our vision. When we cannot walk, He can make us fly.

Goals *for* This Month

He gives strength to the weary and
increases the power of the weak.
ISAIAH 40:29 NIV

January–February 2024

S	M	T	W	T	F	S
					1	2	3
4	5	6	7	8	9	10
11	12	13	14	15	16	17
18	19	20	21	22	23	24
25	26	27	28	29		

God knows you. He knows your intents. And if they're aligned with His, you're good to go. No matter what anyone else thinks or says, you're well equipped in Him to face whatever challenges He's calling you to face.

to-do list

- [ ]
- [ ]
- [ ]
- [ ]
- [ ]
- [ ]
- [ ]
- [ ]
- [ ]
- [ ]
- [ ]
- [ ]
- [ ]
- [ ]
- [ ]
- [ ]
- [ ]
- [ ]

SUNDAY, January 28

MONDAY, January 29

TUESDAY, January 30

WEDNESDAY, January 31

THURSDAY, February 1

FRIDAY, February 2

SATURDAY, February 3

- [ ]
- [ ]
- [ ]
- [ ]
- [ ]
- [ ]
- [ ]
- [ ]
- [ ]
- [ ]
- [ ]
- [ ]
- [ ]
- [ ]
- [ ]
- [ ]
- [ ]
- [ ]

"The LORD who delivered me from the paw of the lion and from the paw of the bear will deliver me from the hand of this Philistine."
1 SAMUEL 17:37 ESV

February 2024

S	M	T	W	T	F	S
				1	2	3
4	5	6	7	8	9	10
11	12	13	14	15	16	17
18	19	20	21	22	23	24
25	26	27	28	29		

You have the choice of walking by faith, seeing things from God's perspective, and making that your reality instead of walking by sight and seeing things from a limited human perspective. Today—and every day—remember David and Goliath. And walk by faith.

to-do list

- [ ]
- [ ]
- [ ]
- [ ]
- [ ]
- [ ]
- [ ]
- [ ]
- [ ]
- [ ]
- [ ]
- [ ]
- [ ]
- [ ]
- [ ]
- [ ]
- [ ]
- [ ]

SUNDAY, February 4

MONDAY, February 5

TUESDAY, February 6

WEDNESDAY, February 7

THURSDAY, February 8

FRIDAY, February 9

SATURDAY, February 10

to-do list

- ☐
- ☐
- ☐
- ☐
- ☐
- ☐
- ☐
- ☐
- ☐
- ☐
- ☐
- ☐
- ☐

"You come against me with a dagger, spear, and sword, but I come against you in the name of Yahweh.... Today, the LORD will hand you over to me.... Then all the world will know...that it is not by sword or by spear that the LORD saves, for the battle is the LORD's."
1 SAMUEL 17:45–47 HCSB

February 2024

S	M	T	W	T	F	S
				1	2	3
4	5	6	7	8	9	10
11	12	13	14	15	16	17
18	19	20	21	22	23	24
25	26	27	28	29		

God has given you a spirit of power, love, and self-control. And you need all three to buoy your faith—"the leaning of your entire personality on God in Christ in absolute trust and confidence in His power, wisdom, and goodness" (2 Timothy 1:5 AMPC). That's something worth praying on and working toward.

to-do list

- ☐ ....
- ☐ ....
- ☐ ....
- ☐ ....
- ☐ ....
- ☐ ....
- ☐ ....
- ☐ ....
- ☐ ....
- ☐ ....
- ☐ ....
- ☐ ....
- ☐ ....
- ☐ ....
- ☐ ....
- ☐ ....
- ☐ ....
- ☐ ....

SUNDAY, February 11

....
....
....
....
....

MONDAY, February 12

....
....
....
....
....

TUESDAY, February 13

....
....
....
....
....

WEDNESDAY, February 14

Valentine's Day
Ash Wednesday

....
....
....
....
....

THURSDAY, February 15

....
....
....
....
....
....

FRIDAY, February 16

....
....
....
....
....
....

SATURDAY, February 17

....
....
....
....
....

to-do list

☐ ....
☐ ....
☐ ....
☐ ....
☐ ....
☐ ....
☐ ....
☐ ....
☐ ....
☐ ....
☐ ....
☐ ....
☐ ....
☐ ....

Instantly Jesus reached out His hand and caught and held [Peter], saying to him, O you of little faith, why did you doubt? And when they got into the boat, the wind ceased. And those in the boat knelt and worshiped Him, saying, Truly You are the Son of God!

MATTHEW 14:31–33 AMPC

February 2024

S	M	T	W	T	F	S
				1	2	3
4	5	6	7	8	9	10
11	12	13	14	15	16	17
18	19	20	21	22	23	24
25	26	27	28	29		

One way to fight the fear that arises up within or without is to "trust in the LORD with all your heart, and do not lean on your own understanding. In all your ways acknowledge him, and he will make straight your paths" (Proverbs 3:5–6 ESV).

to-do list

- [ ]
- [ ]
- [ ]
- [ ]
- [ ]
- [ ]
- [ ]
- [ ]
- [ ]
- [ ]
- [ ]
- [ ]
- [ ]
- [ ]
- [ ]
- [ ]
- [ ]
- [ ]

SUNDAY, February 18

MONDAY, February 19   *Presidents' Day*

TUESDAY, February 20

WEDNESDAY, February 21

....
....
....
....
....

THURSDAY, February 22

....
....
....
....
....

FRIDAY, February 23

....
....
....
....
....

SATURDAY, February 24

....
....
....
....
....

to-do list

- [ ] ....
- [ ] ....
- [ ] ....
- [ ] ....
- [ ] ....
- [ ] ....
- [ ] ....
- [ ] ....
- [ ] ....
- [ ] ....
- [ ] ....
- [ ] ....
- [ ] ....
- [ ] ....
- [ ] ....

*So David went back
to GOD in prayer. GOD
said, "Get going."*
1 SAMUEL 23:4 MSG

February–March 2024

S	M	T	W	T	F	S
				1	2	3
4	5	6	7	8	9	10
11	12	13	14	15	16	17
18	19	20	21	22	23	24
25	26	27	28	29		

If you want to be used by God in unique circumstances, pray—not to pull God to your will but to align your will with His. That way, when God does call, you won't be afraid. You'll just get up and go.

to-do list

- [ ]
- [ ]
- [ ]
- [ ]
- [ ]
- [ ]
- [ ]
- [ ]
- [ ]
- [ ]
- [ ]
- [ ]
- [ ]
- [ ]
- [ ]
- [ ]
- [ ]
- [ ]
- [ ]

SUNDAY, February 25

MONDAY, February 26

TUESDAY, February 27

WEDNESDAY, February 28

THURSDAY, February 29   *Leap Day*

FRIDAY, March 1

SATURDAY, March 2

to-do list

- [ ]
- [ ]
- [ ]
- [ ]
- [ ]
- [ ]
- [ ]
- [ ]
- [ ]
- [ ]
- [ ]
- [ ]
- [ ]

I will trust and not be afraid, for the Lord God is my strength and song.... The Lord...has done excellent things [gloriously]; let this be made known to all the earth. Cry aloud and shout joyfully, you women...for great in your midst is the Holy One.
ISAIAH 12:2, 5-6 AMPC

March 2024

SUNDAY	MONDAY	TUESDAY	WEDNESDAY
25	26	27	28
3	4	5	6
10 *Daylight Saving Time Begins*	11	12	13
17 *St. Patrick's Day*	18	19 *First Day of Spring*	20
24 *Easter Sunday* 31	25	26	27

THURSDAY	FRIDAY	SATURDAY
29	1	2
7	8	9
14	15	16
21	22	23
28	29	30
	Good Friday	

notes

....
....
....
....
....
....
....
....
....
....
....
....
....

FEBRUARY

S	M	T	W	T	F	S
				1	2	3
4	5	6	7	8	9	10
11	12	13	14	15	16	17
18	19	20	21	22	23	24
25	26	27	28	29		

APRIL

S	M	T	W	T	F	S
	1	2	3	4	5	6
7	8	9	10	11	12	13
14	15	16	17	18	19	20
21	22	23	24	25	26	27
28	29	30				

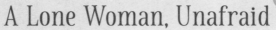

A Lone Woman, Unafraid

God knows there will be times when, like Abigail, we need to stay calm, cool, and collected when called to protect our household. We need to find a way of making peace with others while trusting God to guard and guide us as we seek His wisdom and grace. In doing so, we can have confidence that God will reward our courage in ways beyond our imagining.

Goals *for* This Month

She saw David and his men coming toward her and met them.... When Abigail saw David, she quickly got off the donkey and fell with her face to the ground.
1 SAMUEL 25:20, 23 HCSB

March 2024

S	M	T	W	T	F	S
					1	2
3	4	5	6	7	8	9
10	11	12	13	14	15	16
17	18	19	20	21	22	23
24	25	26	27	28	29	30
31						

Never fear or falter. Ground your life on the Word, knowing that no matter what, Jesus will always seek out your company. He'll still care and provide. He'll tell you to have no fear but simply to follow Him.

to-do list

- ☐
- ☐
- ☐
- ☐
- ☐
- ☐
- ☐
- ☐
- ☐
- ☐
- ☐
- ☐
- ☐
- ☐
- ☐
- ☐
- ☐
- ☐
- ☐
- ☐

SUNDAY, March 3

MONDAY, March 4

TUESDAY, March 5

WEDNESDAY, March 6

THURSDAY, March 7

FRIDAY, March 8

SATURDAY, March 9

Put out into the deep [water], and lower your nets for a haul. And Simon (Peter) answered, Master, we toiled all night [exhaustingly] and caught nothing [in our nets]. But on the ground of Your word, I will lower the nets [again].
LUKE 5:4–5 AMPC

March 2024

S	M	T	W	T	F	S
					1	2
3	4	5	6	7	8	9
10	11	12	13	14	15	16
17	18	19	20	21	22	23
24	25	26	27	28	29	30
31						

During those times when you fear that everyone is against you, go to God. Spend time in His presence. Ask Him what your next steps should be. Allow God to reenergize you, to give you the strength and courage you need to do whatever He would have you do.

to-do list

- [ ]
- [ ]
- [ ]
- [ ]
- [ ]
- [ ]
- [ ]
- [ ]
- [ ]
- [ ]
- [ ]
- [ ]
- [ ]
- [ ]
- [ ]
- [ ]
- [ ]
- [ ]

SUNDAY, March 10   *Daylight Saving Time Begins*

MONDAY, March 11

TUESDAY, March 12

WEDNESDAY, March 13

....
....
....
....
....

THURSDAY, March 14

....
....
....
....
....

FRIDAY, March 15

....
....
....
....
....

SATURDAY, March 16

....
....
....
....
....

to-do list

- [ ] ....
- [ ] ....
- [ ] ....
- [ ] ....
- [ ] ....
- [ ] ....
- [ ] ....
- [ ] ....
- [ ] ....
- [ ] ....
- [ ] ....
- [ ] ....
- [ ] ....
- [ ] ....
- [ ] ....
- [ ] ....

*But David encouraged
and strengthened
himself in the
Lord his God.*
1 SAMUEL 30:6 AMPC

March 2024

S	M	T	W	T	F	S
					1	2
3	4	5	6	7	8	9
10	11	12	13	14	15	16
17	18	19	20	21	22	23
24	25	26	27	28	29	30
31						

No matter how bleak things look, God sees what's happening. Know that He will bring His loving-kindness your way. Your job is to wait patiently—and be strong and hopeful, knowing that God has a plan.

to-do list

- ☐ ....
- ☐ ....
- ☐ ....
- ☐ ....
- ☐ ....
- ☐ ....
- ☐ ....
- ☐ ....
- ☐ ....
- ☐ ....
- ☐ ....
- ☐ ....
- ☐ ....
- ☐ ....
- ☐ ....
- ☐ ....
- ☐ ....
- ☐ ....

SUNDAY, March 17   *St. Patrick's Day*

....

....

....

....

....

MONDAY, March 18

....

....

....

....

....

TUESDAY, March 19   *First Day of Spring*

....

....

....

....

....

WEDNESDAY, March 20

THURSDAY, March 21

FRIDAY, March 22

SATURDAY, March 23

to-do list

☐
☐
☐
☐
☐
☐
☐
☐
☐
☐
☐
☐
☐
☐

[What, what would have become of me] had I not believed that I would see the Lord's goodness in the land of the living! Wait and hope for and expect the Lord; be brave and of good courage and let your heart be stout and enduring.
PSALM 27:13–14 AMPC

March 2024

S	M	T	W	T	F	S
					1	2
3	4	5	6	7	8	9
10	11	12	13	14	15	16
17	18	19	20	21	22	23
24	25	26	27	28	29	30
31						

Daughter of God, sister of Jesus, you need not be afraid to step out, to do what God calls you to do. God is with you. He will never leave you. He will fulfill His promises to you when you step out in faith, in Him (see Luke 1:45).

to-do list

- [ ]
- [ ]
- [ ]
- [ ]
- [ ]
- [ ]
- [ ]
- [ ]
- [ ]
- [ ]
- [ ]
- [ ]
- [ ]
- [ ]
- [ ]
- [ ]
- [ ]
- [ ]
- [ ]

SUNDAY, March 24   *Palm Sunday*

MONDAY, March 25

TUESDAY, March 26

WEDNESDAY, March 27

THURSDAY, March 28

FRIDAY, March 29   *Good Friday*

SATURDAY, March 30

to-do list

☐
☐
☐
☐
☐
☐
☐
☐
☐
☐
☐
☐
☐

Do you not discern and understand that you [the whole church at Corinth] are God's temple (His sanctuary), and that God's Spirit has His permanent dwelling in you [to be at home in you, collectively as a church and also individually]?

1 CORINTHIANS 3:16 AMPC

April 2024

SUNDAY	MONDAY	TUESDAY	WEDNESDAY
31	1	2	3
7	8	9	10
14	15	16	17
21	22 *Passover Begins at Sundown*	23	24
28	29	30	1

THURSDAY	FRIDAY	SATURDAY
4	5	6
11	12	13
18	19	20
25	26	27
2	3	4

....
....
....
....
....
....
....
....
....
....
....

MARCH

S	M	T	W	T	F	S
					1	2
3	4	5	6	7	8	9
10	11	12	13	14	15	16
17	18	19	20	21	22	23
24	25	26	27	28	29	30
31						

MAY

S	M	T	W	T	F	S
			1	2	3	4
5	6	7	8	9	10	11
12	13	14	15	16	17	18
19	20	21	22	23	24	25
26	27	28	29	30	31	

From Storm Wind
to Whisper

If we've experienced a whirlwind of emotions, riding a roller coaster through personal drama, God will still our storms. He will hush the hysterical outpourings of our hearts and turn down the volume on the drama. He will quiet our wind to a whisper so we can finally hear Him speak.

Goals *for* This Month

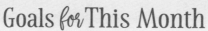

He quieted the wind down to a whisper,
put a muzzle on all the big waves.
PSALM 107:29 MSG

March-April 2024

S	M	T	W	T	F	S
					1	2
3	4	5	6	7	8	9
7	8	9	10	11	12	13
14	15	16	17	18	19	20
21	22	23	24	25	26	27
28	29	30				

God is with you. He values you, knows you like no other. When you're feeling afraid, alone, deserted, ignored, unfriended, neglected, and rejected, get closer to God. Value Him as much as He values you.

to-do list

- [ ] ....
- [ ] ....
- [ ] ....
- [ ] ....
- [ ] ....
- [ ] ....
- [ ] ....
- [ ] ....
- [ ] ....
- [ ] ....
- [ ] ....
- [ ] ....
- [ ] ....
- [ ] ....
- [ ] ....
- [ ] ....
- [ ] ....

SUNDAY, March 31   *Easter*

MONDAY, April 1

TUESDAY, April 2

WEDNESDAY, April 3

THURSDAY, April 4

FRIDAY, April 5

SATURDAY, April 6

to-do list

- [ ]
- [ ]
- [ ]
- [ ]
- [ ]
- [ ]
- [ ]
- [ ]
- [ ]
- [ ]
- [ ]
- [ ]
- [ ]

Are not five sparrows sold for two pennies? And [yet] not one of them is forgotten or uncared for in the presence of God. But [even] the very hairs of your head are all numbered. Do not be struck with fear or seized with alarm; you are of greater worth than many [flocks] of sparrows.
LUKE 12:6–7 AMPC

April 2024

S	M	T	W	T	F	S
	1	2	3	4	5	6
7	8	9	10	11	12	13
14	15	16	17	18	19	20
21	22	23	24	25	26	27
28	29	30				

What does it mean to seek God's kingdom? It means to make God a priority in your life, to seek Him early in the morning through prayer and reading of the Word. To search for His presence, wisdom, will, and way. As you do so, worries and fears will fade away.

to-do list

- [ ] ....
- [ ] ....
- [ ] ....
- [ ] ....
- [ ] ....
- [ ] ....
- [ ] ....
- [ ] ....
- [ ] ....
- [ ] ....
- [ ] ....
- [ ] ....
- [ ] ....
- [ ] ....
- [ ] ....
- [ ] ....
- [ ] ....
- [ ] ....
- [ ] ....

SUNDAY, April 7

MONDAY, April 8

TUESDAY, April 9

WEDNESDAY, April 10

THURSDAY, April 11

FRIDAY, April 12

SATURDAY, April 13

- [ ]
- [ ]
- [ ]
- [ ]
- [ ]
- [ ]
- [ ]
- [ ]
- [ ]
- [ ]
- [ ]

"Do not seek what you are to eat and what you are to drink, nor be worried. For all...seek after these things, and your Father knows that you need them. Instead, seek his kingdom, and these things will be added to you. Fear not...for it is your Father's good pleasure to give you the kingdom."
LUKE 12:29–32 ESV

April 2024

S	M	T	W	T	F	S
	1	2	3	4	5	6
7	8	9	10	11	12	13
14	15	16	17	18	19	20
21	22	23	24	25	26	27
28	29	30				

Remember that God knows exactly who you are and what you need. He knows your weaknesses and fears, your assets and your liabilities. And God will use all those things to demonstrate His power and strength as He works through you!

to-do list

- [ ]
- [ ]
- [ ]
- [ ]
- [ ]
- [ ]
- [ ]
- [ ]
- [ ]
- [ ]
- [ ]
- [ ]
- [ ]
- [ ]
- [ ]
- [ ]
- [ ]
- [ ]

SUNDAY, April 14

MONDAY, April 15

TUESDAY, April 16

WEDNESDAY, April 17

....
....
....
....
....

THURSDAY, April 18

....
....
....
....
....

FRIDAY, April 19

....
....
....
....
....

SATURDAY, April 20

....
....
....
....
....

to-do list

☐ ....
☐ ....
☐ ....
☐ ....
☐ ....
☐ ....
☐ ....
☐ ....
☐ ....
☐ ....
☐ ....
☐ ....
☐ ....
☐ ....
☐ ....
☐ ....

*He answered me,
"I am all you need. I
give you My loving-
favor. My power
works best in weak
people." I am happy
to be weak and have
troubles so I can have
Christ's power in me.*
2 CORINTHIANS 12:9 NLV

April 2024

S	M	T	W	T	F	S
	1	2	3	4	5	6
7	8	9	10	11	12	13
14	15	16	17	18	19	20
21	22	23	24	25	26	27
28	29	30				

Perhaps God is preparing you, an ordinary woman, to play an extraordinary part. In doing so, He wants you to learn how to keep calm amid chaos, to be steadfast when trouble comes. With God at your center, you will not fail.

to-do list

- [ ] ....
- [ ] ....
- [ ] ....
- [ ] ....
- [ ] ....
- [ ] ....
- [ ] ....
- [ ] ....
- [ ] ....
- [ ] ....
- [ ] ....
- [ ] ....
- [ ] ....
- [ ] ....
- [ ] ....
- [ ] ....
- [ ] ....
- [ ] ....
- [ ] ....

SUNDAY, April 21

MONDAY, April 22   *Passover Begins at Sundown*

TUESDAY, April 23

WEDNESDAY, April 24

....
....
....
....
....

THURSDAY, April 25

....
....
....
....
....

FRIDAY, April 26

....
....
....
....
....

SATURDAY, April 27

....
....
....
....
....

to-do list

- [ ] ....
- [ ] ....
- [ ] ....
- [ ] ....
- [ ] ....
- [ ] ....
- [ ] ....
- [ ] ....
- [ ] ....
- [ ] ....
- [ ] ....
- [ ] ....
- [ ] ....
- [ ] ....
- [ ] ....
- [ ] ....

God is in the center of her. She will not be moved. God will help her when the morning comes.... The Lord of All is with us. The God of Jacob is our strong place.
PSALM 46:5, 11 NLV

May 2024

SUNDAY	MONDAY	TUESDAY	WEDNESDAY
28	29	30	1
5	6	7	8
12 *Mother's Day*	13	14	15
19	20	21	22
26	27 *Memorial Day*	28	29

THURSDAY	FRIDAY	SATURDAY
2 National Day of Prayer	3	4
9	10	11
16	17	18
23	24	25
30	31	1

APRIL

S	M	T	W	T	F	S
		1	2	3	4	5	6
7	8	9	10	11	12	13
14	15	16	17	18	19	20
21	22	23	24	25	26	27
28	29	30				

JUNE

S	M	T	W	T	F	S
						1
2	3	4	5	6	7	8
9	10	11	12	13	14	15
16	17	18	19	20	21	22
23	24	25	26	27	28	29
30						

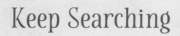

Keep Searching

Jesus wants you to know, to get it straight in your head, that when you continue to come to Father God, to ask, seek, and knock on His door, "He will not drag his feet" (Luke 18:8 MSG) to help you. So don't "turn coward (faint, lose heart, and give up)" (Luke 18:1 AMPC). Keep on asking, searching, and knocking, knowing that God will, in His perfect time, answer the prayer of the persistent.

Goals for This Month

"So I say to you, keep asking, and it will be given to you. Keep searching, and you will find. Keep knocking, and the door will be opened to you. For everyone who asks receives, and the one who searches finds, and to the one who knocks, the door will be opened."

LUKE 11:9–10 HCSB

April–May 2024

S	M	T	W	T	F	S
				1	2	3	4
5	6	7	8	9	10	11
12	13	14	15	16	17	18
19	20	21	22	23	24	25
26	27	28	29	30	31	

You can be part of God's amazing story—if you replace your fears with faith. If you live focused on the unseen rather than the seen. If you become sure of receiving the things you hope for, certain they exist even though you cannot yet see them. Believe!

to-do list

- [ ]
- [ ]
- [ ]
- [ ]
- [ ]
- [ ]
- [ ]
- [ ]
- [ ]
- [ ]
- [ ]
- [ ]
- [ ]
- [ ]
- [ ]
- [ ]
- [ ]
- [ ]
- [ ]

SUNDAY, April 28

MONDAY, April 29

TUESDAY, April 30

WEDNESDAY, May 1

....
....
....
....
....

THURSDAY, May 2   *National Day of Prayer*

....
....
....
....
....

FRIDAY, May 3

....
....
....
....
....

SATURDAY, May 4

....
....
....
....
....

to-do list

☐ ....
☐ ....
☐ ....
☐ ....
☐ ....
☐ ....
☐ ....
☐ ....
☐ ....
☐ ....
☐ ....
☐ ....
☐ ....
☐ ....
☐ ....
☐ ....

*Our life is lived by faith.
We do not live by what
we see in front of us....
Now faith is being sure
we will get what we hope
for. It is being sure of
what we cannot see.*
2 CORINTHIANS 5:7;
HEBREWS 11:1 NLV

May 2024

S	M	T	W	T	F	S
			1	2	3	4
5	6	7	8	9	10	11
12	13	14	15	16	17	18
19	20	21	22	23	24	25
26	27	28	29	30	31	

God is *still* in the business of answering prayers. And right now He's waiting for yours. So take to God all your worries, concerns, and problems—big and small. Cry out to Him with groans, moans, or words, and know that He will hear. He will answer.

to-do list

- ☐
- ☐
- ☐
- ☐
- ☐
- ☐
- ☐
- ☐
- ☐
- ☐
- ☐
- ☐
- ☐
- ☐
- ☐
- ☐
- ☐
- ☐

SUNDAY, May 5

MONDAY, May 6

TUESDAY, May 7

WEDNESDAY, May 8

THURSDAY, May 9

FRIDAY, May 10

SATURDAY, May 11

☐
☐
☐
☐
☐
☐
☐
☐
☐
☐
☐
☐
☐
☐

As for God, His way is perfect; the word of the Lord is tried. He is a Shield to all those who trust and take refuge in Him.... God is my strong Fortress; He guides the blameless in His way and sets him free.... He sets me secure and confident upon the heights.

2 SAMUEL 22:31, 33–34 AMPC

May 2024

S	M	T	W	T	F	S
			1	2	3	4
5	6	7	8	9	10	11
12	13	14	15	16	17	18
19	20	21	22	23	24	25
26	27	28	29	30	31	

It's not wrong to enjoy our lives. But focusing too much on what happens to us in the here and now may result in our losing sight of the yet to come. And God has so much more in store for us!

to-do list

☐ ....
☐ ....
☐ ....
☐ ....
☐ ....
☐ ....
☐ ....
☐ ....
☐ ....
☐ ....
☐ ....
☐ ....
☐ ....
☐ ....
☐ ....
☐ ....
☐ ....
☐ ....

SUNDAY, May 12   *Mother's Day*

....
....
....
....
....

MONDAY, May 13

....
....
....
....
....

TUESDAY, May 14

....
....
....
....
....

WEDNESDAY, May 15

....
....
....
....
....

THURSDAY, May 16

....
....
....
....
....

FRIDAY, May 17

....
....
....
....
....

SATURDAY, May 18

....
....
....
....
....

to-do list

☐ ....
☐ ....
☐ ....
☐ ....
☐ ....
☐ ....
☐ ....
☐ ....
☐ ....
☐ ....
☐ ....
☐ ....
☐ ....
☐ ....
☐ ....
☐ ....

"Anyone who loves their life will lose it, while anyone who hates their life in this world will keep it for eternal life."
JOHN 12:25 NIV

May 2024

S	M	T	W	T	F	S
			1	2	3	4
5	6	7	8	9	10	11
12	13	14	15	16	17	18
19	20	21	22	23	24	25
26	27	28	29	30	31	

Our Lord is mighty and powerful. He can give us strength. He can reach into our hearts and mend our wounds. He can see into our minds and help us untangle the knots. God will not always stop the floods from coming. But He will always be with us in the water.

to-do list

- [ ] ....
- [ ] ....
- [ ] ....
- [ ] ....
- [ ] ....
- [ ] ....
- [ ] ....
- [ ] ....
- [ ] ....
- [ ] ....
- [ ] ....
- [ ] ....
- [ ] ....
- [ ] ....
- [ ] ....
- [ ] ....
- [ ] ....
- [ ] ....
- [ ] ....
- [ ] ....

SUNDAY, May 19

MONDAY, May 20

TUESDAY, May 21

WEDNESDAY, May 22

THURSDAY, May 23

FRIDAY, May 24

SATURDAY, May 25

to-do list

- [ ] ....
- [ ] ....
- [ ] ....
- [ ] ....
- [ ] ....
- [ ] ....
- [ ] ....
- [ ] ....
- [ ] ....
- [ ] ....
- [ ] ....
- [ ] ....
- [ ] ....
- [ ] ....
- [ ] ....
- [ ] ....
- [ ] ....
- [ ] ....

The LORD sits enthroned over the flood; the LORD is enthroned as King forever. The LORD gives strength to his people; the LORD blesses his people with peace.
PSALM 29:10-11 NIV

May–June 2024

S	M	T	W	T	F	S
			1	2	3	4
5	6	7	8	9	10	11
12	13	14	15	16	17	18
19	20	21	22	23	24	25
26	27	28	29	30	31	

God loves it when you're trusting in Him, following where your curiosity leads, being fearless in new situations. What God hates is when confidence turns to criticism or cockiness. Today, examine your own walk with God. Where might He want you to be humbler and more encouraging?

to-do list

- [ ] ....
- [ ] ....
- [ ] ....
- [ ] ....
- [ ] ....
- [ ] ....
- [ ] ....
- [ ] ....
- [ ] ....
- [ ] ....
- [ ] ....
- [ ] ....
- [ ] ....
- [ ] ....
- [ ] ....
- [ ] ....
- [ ] ....
- [ ] ....
- [ ] ....

SUNDAY, May 26

MONDAY, May 27 *Memorial Day*

TUESDAY, May 28

WEDNESDAY, May 29

THURSDAY, May 30

FRIDAY, May 31

SATURDAY, June 1

- [ ]
- [ ]
- [ ]
- [ ]
- [ ]
- [ ]
- [ ]
- [ ]
- [ ]
- [ ]
- [ ]
- [ ]
- [ ]
- [ ]
- [ ]
- [ ]
- [ ]

*"I brought you out of the
land of Egypt.... And I
sent Moses, Aaron and
Miriam to lead you."*
MICAH 6:4 NLV

June 2024

SUNDAY	MONDAY	TUESDAY	WEDNESDAY
26	27	28	29
2	3	4	5
9	10	11	12
16	17	18	19
23 *Father's Day* / 30	24	25	26

THURSDAY	FRIDAY	SATURDAY
30	31	1
6	7	8
13	14 *Flag Day*	15
20 *First Day of Summer*	21	22
27	28	29

notes

....
....
....
....
....
....
....
....
....
....
....
....
....

MAY

S	M	T	W	T	F	S
			1	2	3	4
5	6	7	8	9	10	11
12	13	14	15	16	17	18
19	20	21	22	23	24	25
26	27	28	29	30	31	

JULY

S	M	T	W	T	F	S
	1	2	3	4	5	6
7	8	9	10	11	12	13
14	15	16	17	18	19	20
21	22	23	24	25	26	27
28	29	30	31			

Never Separated

The truth is, we all need to be reminded that we are not alone. That we are never ever alone. That nothing can separate us from the love of good people, and nothing can keep us away from the love of Christ. No troubles. No bumps in the night. No bad people. No illness. No persecution. No physical conditions. No mental conditions. No demons. No distance. Absolutely nothing can keep us from God's eternal, powerful, pure, forgiving love.

Goals *for* This Month

For I am convinced that neither death nor life, neither angels nor demons, neither the present nor the future, nor any powers, neither height nor depth, nor anything else in all creation, will be able to separate us from the love of God that is in Christ Jesus our Lord.
ROMANS 8:38–39 NIV

June 2024

S	M	T	W	T	F	S
						1
2	3	4	5	6	7	8
9	10	11	12	13	14	15
16	17	18	19	20	21	22
23	24	25	26	27	28	29
30						

God can and will use you—no matter what you look like or feel like, or what your life has been like to this point. And not only will He use you to do great things in His kingdom, but He also loves you.

to-do list

- [ ] ....
- [ ] ....
- [ ] ....
- [ ] ....
- [ ] ....
- [ ] ....
- [ ] ....
- [ ] ....
- [ ] ....
- [ ] ....
- [ ] ....
- [ ] ....
- [ ] ....
- [ ] ....
- [ ] ....
- [ ] ....
- [ ] ....
- [ ] ....

SUNDAY, June 2

MONDAY, June 3

TUESDAY, June 4

WEDNESDAY, June 5

THURSDAY, June 6

FRIDAY, June 7

SATURDAY, June 8

to-do list

- [ ]
- [ ]
- [ ]
- [ ]
- [ ]
- [ ]
- [ ]
- [ ]
- [ ]
- [ ]
- [ ]
- [ ]
- [ ]
- [ ]
- [ ]
- [ ]
- [ ]
- [ ]
- [ ]

*I will call Not My People,
My People, and she who
is Unloved, Beloved.*
ROMANS 9:25 CSB

June 2024

S	M	T	W	T	F	S
						1
2	3	4	5	6	7	8
9	10	11	12	13	14	15
16	17	18	19	20	21	22
23	24	25	26	27	28	29
30						

When you're exhausted mentally, physically, emotionally, and spiritually, fear can find a foothold in you. That's when you need to find a place to be alone with God, allowing Him to recharge and redirect you, giving you the courage to walk His way.

to-do list

- [ ] ....
- [ ] ....
- [ ] ....
- [ ] ....
- [ ] ....
- [ ] ....
- [ ] ....
- [ ] ....
- [ ] ....
- [ ] ....
- [ ] ....
- [ ] ....
- [ ] ....
- [ ] ....
- [ ] ....
- [ ] ....
- [ ] ....
- [ ] ....
- [ ] ....

SUNDAY, June 9

MONDAY, June 10

TUESDAY, June 11

WEDNESDAY, June 12

....
....
....
....
....

THURSDAY, June 13

....
....
....
....
....

FRIDAY, June 14   *Flag Day*

....
....
....
....
....

SATURDAY, June 15

....
....
....
....
....

to-do list

- [ ] ....
- [ ] ....
- [ ] ....
- [ ] ....
- [ ] ....
- [ ] ....
- [ ] ....
- [ ] ....
- [ ] ....
- [ ] ....
- [ ] ....
- [ ] ....
- [ ] ....

The LORD was not in the wind. After the wind there was an earthquake, but the LORD was not in the earthquake. After the earthquake there was a fire, but the LORD was not in the fire. And after the fire there was a voice, a soft whisper.
1 KINGS 19:11–12 HCSB

June 2024

S	M	T	W	T	F	S
						1
2	3	4	5	6	7	8
9	10	11	12	13	14	15
16	17	18	19	20	21	22
23	24	25	26	27	28	29
30						

to-do list

- [ ]
- [ ]
- [ ]
- [ ]
- [ ]
- [ ]
- [ ]
- [ ]
- [ ]
- [ ]
- [ ]
- [ ]
- [ ]
- [ ]
- [ ]
- [ ]
- [ ]
- [ ]

We can praise God with sounds of celebration, and we can praise Him with our loudness. In all the sounds of our human emotions, we can praise the God who gives us every breath—the God who is with us even before we take in air at birth for our first breath, and the God who waits for us as we exhale our last.

SUNDAY, June 16   *Father's Day*

MONDAY, June 17

TUESDAY, June 18

WEDNESDAY, June 19

THURSDAY, June 20   *First Day of Summer*

FRIDAY, June 21

SATURDAY, June 22

to-do list

☐
☐
☐
☐
☐
☐
☐
☐
☐
☐
☐
☐
☐
☐
☐
☐
☐

*Let everything that has
breath praise the LORD.*
PSALM 150:6 NIV

June 2024

S	M	T	W	T	F	S
						1
2	3	4	5	6	7	8
9	10	11	12	13	14	15
16	17	18	19	20	21	22
23	24	25	26	27	28	29
30						

When fear and anxiety threaten to overtake you, cry out to God. Open your heart. Give God what you have. Believe for the impossible. Garner God's strength. Obey God's instructions. And you will witness a miracle.

to-do list

- [ ]
- [ ]
- [ ]
- [ ]
- [ ]
- [ ]
- [ ]
- [ ]
- [ ]
- [ ]
- [ ]
- [ ]
- [ ]
- [ ]
- [ ]
- [ ]
- [ ]
- [ ]

SUNDAY, June 23

MONDAY, June 24

TUESDAY, June 25

WEDNESDAY, June 26

THURSDAY, June 27

FRIDAY, June 28

SATURDAY, June 29

to-do list

☐ ....
☐ ....
☐ ....
☐ ....
☐ ....
☐ ....
☐ ....
☐ ....
☐ ....
☐ ....
☐ ....
☐ ....
☐ ....

I have begun shaking with fear. Fear has power over me.... I will call on God and the Lord will save me.... Give all your cares to the Lord and He will give you strength. He will never let those who are right with Him be shaken.
PSALM 55:5, 16, 22 NLV

July 2024

SUNDAY	MONDAY	TUESDAY	WEDNESDAY
30	1	2	3
7	8	9	10
14	15	16	17
21	22	23	24
28	29	30	31

THURSDAY	FRIDAY	SATURDAY
4	5	6
Independence Day		
11	12	13
18	19	20
25	26	27
1	2	3

notes

....
....
....
....
....
....
....
....
....
....
....
....
....
....
....
....

JUNE

S	M	T	W	T	F	S
						1
2	3	4	5	6	7	8
9	10	11	12	13	14	15
16	17	18	19	20	21	22
23	24	25	26	27	28	29
30						

AUGUST

S	M	T	W	T	F	S
				1	2	3
4	5	6	7	8	9	10
11	12	13	14	15	16	17
18	19	20	21	22	23	24
25	26	27	28	29	30	31

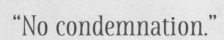

"No condemnation."

Consider those two words to be your life slogan. How is your life different, or how should it be different, with the knowledge that you are free from condemnation? You never have to face hell, because Jesus faced it for you. You can know without a doubt that your life here on earth is just a dot on an eternal line, and you get to live out the rest of that line in the freedom and glory of heaven.

Goals *for* This Month

*There is therefore now no condemnation to those
who are in Christ Jesus, who do not walk according
to the flesh, but according to the Spirit.*
ROMANS 8:1 NKJV

June-July 2024

S	M	T	W	T	F	S
						1
2	3	4	5	6	7	8
7	8	9	10	11	12	13
14	15	16	17	18	19	20
21	22	23	24	25	26	27
28	29	30	31			

God is in charge. Only God. He's the only author of our lives. He's our Creator and our King. And He is good. No matter what we think or do or say, no matter what power we think we might have, the only one who really understands the big picture is God.

to-do list

- [ ] ....
- [ ] ....
- [ ] ....
- [ ] ....
- [ ] ....
- [ ] ....
- [ ] ....
- [ ] ....
- [ ] ....
- [ ] ....
- [ ] ....
- [ ] ....
- [ ] ....
- [ ] ....
- [ ] ....
- [ ] ....
- [ ] ....
- [ ] ....

SUNDAY, June 30

MONDAY, July 1

TUESDAY, July 2

WEDNESDAY, July 3

THURSDAY, July 4   *Independence Day*

FRIDAY, July 5

SATURDAY, July 6

- [ ]
- [ ]
- [ ]
- [ ]
- [ ]
- [ ]
- [ ]
- [ ]
- [ ]
- [ ]
- [ ]
- [ ]
- [ ]
- [ ]
- [ ]
- [ ]
- [ ]
- [ ]
- [ ]

*"I have no rest;
only trouble comes."*
JOB 3:26 NLT

July 2024

S	M	T	W	T	F	S
		1	2	3	4	5	6
7	8	9	10	11	12	13
14	15	16	17	18	19	20
21	22	23	24	25	26	27
28	29	30	31			

We should expect opposition. There will be bumps in the road and even whole roadblocks. Have patience. Keep pushing. Keep fighting. Keep reading God's Word. Keep praying. Keep the faith. Run the race.

to-do list

- [ ]
- [ ]
- [ ]
- [ ]
- [ ]
- [ ]
- [ ]
- [ ]
- [ ]
- [ ]
- [ ]
- [ ]
- [ ]
- [ ]
- [ ]
- [ ]
- [ ]
- [ ]

SUNDAY, July 7

MONDAY, July 8

TUESDAY, July 9

WEDNESDAY, July 10

THURSDAY, July 11

FRIDAY, July 12

SATURDAY, July 13

- [ ]
- [ ]
- [ ]
- [ ]
- [ ]
- [ ]
- [ ]
- [ ]
- [ ]
- [ ]
- [ ]
- [ ]
- [ ]
- [ ]
- [ ]
- [ ]
- [ ]
- [ ]

Consider him who endured such opposition from sinners, so that you will not grow weary and lose heart.
HEBREWS 12:3 NIV

July 2024

S	M	T	W	T	F	S
	1	2	3	4	5	6
7	8	9	10	11	12	13
14	15	16	17	18	19	20
21	22	23	24	25	26	27
28	29	30	31			

No matter how anxious or confused or scared we might feel, we can know for certain that when we look around the room, God is there. He is there with us. He is there for us. And He is lighting up, delighted to see us and ready to call out our name.

to-do list

- ☐ ....
- ☐ ....
- ☐ ....
- ☐ ....
- ☐ ....
- ☐ ....
- ☐ ....
- ☐ ....
- ☐ ....
- ☐ ....
- ☐ ....
- ☐ ....
- ☐ ....
- ☐ ....
- ☐ ....
- ☐ ....
- ☐ ....
- ☐ ....
- ☐ ....

SUNDAY, July 14

....
....
....
....
....

MONDAY, July 15

....
....
....
....
....

TUESDAY, July 16

....
....
....
....
....

WEDNESDAY, July 17

THURSDAY, July 18

FRIDAY, July 19

SATURDAY, July 20

to-do list

- [ ] ....
- [ ] ....
- [ ] ....
- [ ] ....
- [ ] ....
- [ ] ....
- [ ] ....
- [ ] ....
- [ ] ....
- [ ] ....
- [ ] ....
- [ ] ....
- [ ] ....
- [ ] ....
- [ ] ....
- [ ] ....
- [ ] ....

"I will grant peace in the land, and you will lie down and no one will make you afraid."
LEVITICUS 26:6 NIV

July 2024

S	M	T	W	T	F	S
		1	2	3	4	5	6
7	8	9	10	11	12	13
14	15	16	17	18	19	20
21	22	23	24	25	26	27
28	29	30	31			

Thanks to God, we can never be lost in His kingdom. Even when we try to hide, He comes to us. He restores us. He reminds us exactly how important we are to Him. And He leads us back to where we need to be going.

to-do list

- [ ]
- [ ]
- [ ]
- [ ]
- [ ]
- [ ]
- [ ]
- [ ]
- [ ]
- [ ]
- [ ]
- [ ]
- [ ]
- [ ]
- [ ]
- [ ]
- [ ]
- [ ]

SUNDAY, July 21

MONDAY, July 22

TUESDAY, July 23

WEDNESDAY, July 24

....
....
....
....
....

THURSDAY, July 25

....
....
....
....
....

FRIDAY, July 26

....
....
....
....
....

SATURDAY, July 27

....
....
....
....
....

to-do list

- [ ] ....
- [ ] ....
- [ ] ....
- [ ] ....
- [ ] ....
- [ ] ....
- [ ] ....
- [ ] ....
- [ ] ....
- [ ] ....
- [ ] ....
- [ ] ....
- [ ] ....
- [ ] ....
- [ ] ....

*"And when she finds it,
she calls her friends and
neighbors together and
says, 'Rejoice with me;
I have found my lost coin.'"*
LUKE 15:9 NIV

August 2024

SUNDAY	MONDAY	TUESDAY	WEDNESDAY
28	29	30	31
4	5	6	7
11	12	13	14
18	19	20	21
25	26	27	28

THURSDAY	FRIDAY	SATURDAY
1	2	3
8	9	10
15	16	17
22	23	24
29	30	31

notes

....
....
....
....
....
....
....
....
....
....
....
....
....

JULY

S	M	T	W	T	F	S
		1	2	3	4	5	6
7	8	9	10	11	12	13
14	15	16	17	18	19	20
21	22	23	24	25	26	27
28	29	30	31			

SEPTEMBER

S	M	T	W	T	F	S
1	2	3	4	5	6	7
8	9	10	11	12	13	14
15	16	17	18	19	20	21
22	23	24	25	26	27	28
29	30					

Just a Little More

When night comes, go out and sit under the sky. Ask God where
He is sending you. Talk to Him about His promises that you read in
His Word. Then look up into the vast field of stars and start count-
ing. And with every star, begin to trust God just a little bit more.

Goals *for* This Month

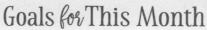

"Look up at the sky and count the stars—if indeed you can count them." Then he said to him, "So shall your offspring be."
GENESIS 15:5 NIV

July–August 2024

S	M	T	W	T	F	S
		1	2	3		
				1	2	3
4	5	6	7	8	9	10
11	12	13	14	15	16	17
18	19	20	21	22	23	24
25	26	27	28	29	30	31

We can be the hands and feet of Jesus. We can bring love to those who need to be held. We can speak truth to those who are confused and wondering. We can give medicine and food and shelter to those who are in need. We can comfort those who are mourning. And we can remind every person that God sees them and knows them by name.

to-do list

- [ ] ....
- [ ] ....
- [ ] ....
- [ ] ....
- [ ] ....
- [ ] ....
- [ ] ....
- [ ] ....
- [ ] ....
- [ ] ....
- [ ] ....
- [ ] ....
- [ ] ....
- [ ] ....
- [ ] ....
- [ ] ....
- [ ] ....
- [ ] ....

SUNDAY, July 28

MONDAY, July 29

TUESDAY, July 30

WEDNESDAY, July 31

THURSDAY, August 1

FRIDAY, August 2

SATURDAY, August 3

to-do list

- [ ]
- [ ]
- [ ]
- [ ]
- [ ]
- [ ]
- [ ]
- [ ]
- [ ]
- [ ]
- [ ]
- [ ]
- [ ]
- [ ]
- [ ]
- [ ]

The LORD is a refuge for the oppressed, a stronghold in times of trouble.
PSALM 9:9 NIV

August 2024

S	M	T	W	T	F	S
				1	2	3
4	5	6	7	8	9	10
11	12	13	14	15	16	17
18	19	20	21	22	23	24
25	26	27	28	29	30	31

Get on your knees and pray. Remind God and yourself of His promises and power. Tell Him that your eyes are on Him alone—and then actually *look* to Him alone! Focus on God by being present *with* Him. Concentrate on Him, looking to see—knowing that you *will* see—Him move on your behalf.

to-do list

- [ ] ....
- [ ] ....
- [ ] ....
- [ ] ....
- [ ] ....
- [ ] ....
- [ ] ....
- [ ] ....
- [ ] ....
- [ ] ....
- [ ] ....
- [ ] ....
- [ ] ....
- [ ] ....
- [ ] ....
- [ ] ....
- [ ] ....
- [ ] ....

SUNDAY, August 4

MONDAY, August 5

TUESDAY, August 6

WEDNESDAY, August 7

THURSDAY, August 8

FRIDAY, August 9

SATURDAY, August 10

to-do list

- [ ]
- [ ]
- [ ]
- [ ]
- [ ]
- [ ]
- [ ]
- [ ]
- [ ]
- [ ]
- [ ]
- [ ]
- [ ]
- [ ]
- [ ]
- [ ]
- [ ]
- [ ]

We have no might to stand against this great company that is coming against us. We do not know what to do, but our eyes are upon You.
2 CHRONICLES 20:12 AMPC

August 2024

S	M	T	W	T	F	S
				1	2	3
4	5	6	7	8	9	10
11	12	13	14	15	16	17
18	19	20	21	22	23	24
25	26	27	28	29	30	31

Muster all your faith, knowing that your Lord is the God of the impossible. Believe He will make a way where there seems to be none. And begin to praise God—no matter how things look or what others say. Know that He will move on your behalf.

to-do list

- [ ]
- [ ]
- [ ]
- [ ]
- [ ]
- [ ]
- [ ]
- [ ]
- [ ]
- [ ]
- [ ]
- [ ]
- [ ]
- [ ]
- [ ]
- [ ]
- [ ]
- [ ]

SUNDAY, August 11

MONDAY, August 12

TUESDAY, August 13

WEDNESDAY, August 14

THURSDAY, August 15

FRIDAY, August 16

SATURDAY, August 17

to-do list

☐
☐
☐
☐
☐
☐
☐
☐
☐
☐
☐
☐
☐
☐
☐
☐
☐

"Do not be afraid or discouraged. Tomorrow, go out to face them, for Yahweh is with you."
2 CHRONICLES 20:17 HCSB

August 2024

S	M	T	W	T	F	S
				1	2	3
4	5	6	7	8	9	10
11	12	13	14	15	16	17
18	19	20	21	22	23	24
25	26	27	28	29	30	31

All through the night, God will watch over you. He will bring you out of darkness with the light of the sun or the light of the moon, or even with the Light of His Son. He will watch you come and go, today and tomorrow and forever.

to-do list

- [ ]
- [ ]
- [ ]
- [ ]
- [ ]
- [ ]
- [ ]
- [ ]
- [ ]
- [ ]
- [ ]
- [ ]
- [ ]
- [ ]
- [ ]
- [ ]
- [ ]
- [ ]

SUNDAY, August 18

MONDAY, August 19

TUESDAY, August 20

WEDNESDAY, August 21

- [ ]
- [ ]
- [ ]
- [ ]
- [ ]
- [ ]
- [ ]
- [ ]
- [ ]
- [ ]
- [ ]
- [ ]
- [ ]
- [ ]
- [ ]
- [ ]

THURSDAY, August 22

FRIDAY, August 23

SATURDAY, August 24

*I lift up my eyes to the
mountains—where does
my help come from?*
PSALM 121:1 NIV

August 2024

S	M	T	W	T	F	S
				1	2	3
4	5	6	7	8	9	10
11	12	13	14	15	16	17
18	19	20	21	22	23	24
25	26	27	28	29	30	31

God does not need our gifts. God does not need anything. But we need to give to Him. We need to be placed in a position of gratitude—to practice offering up something of ourselves for something that is bigger than us.

to-do list

- [ ]
- [ ]
- [ ]
- [ ]
- [ ]
- [ ]
- [ ]
- [ ]
- [ ]
- [ ]
- [ ]
- [ ]
- [ ]
- [ ]
- [ ]
- [ ]
- [ ]
- [ ]

SUNDAY, August 25

MONDAY, August 26

TUESDAY, August 27

WEDNESDAY, August 28

THURSDAY, August 29

FRIDAY, August 30

SATURDAY, August 31

- [ ]
- [ ]
- [ ]
- [ ]
- [ ]
- [ ]
- [ ]
- [ ]
- [ ]
- [ ]
- [ ]
- [ ]
- [ ]
- [ ]
- [ ]
- [ ]
- [ ]
- [ ]

For from him and through him and for him are all things.
ROMANS 11:36 NIV

September 2024

SUNDAY	MONDAY	TUESDAY	WEDNESDAY
1	2 *Labor Day*	3	4
8	9	10	11
15	16	17	18
22	23	24	25
29 *First Day of Autumn*	30	1	2

THURSDAY	FRIDAY	SATURDAY
5	6	7
12	13	14
19	20	21
26	27	28
3	4	5

notes

....
....
....
....
....
....
....
....
....
....
....
....

AUGUST

S	M	T	W	T	F	S
					1	2	3
4	5	6	7	8	9	10
11	12	13	14	15	16	17
18	19	20	21	22	23	24
25	26	27	28	29	30	31

OCTOBER

S	M	T	W	T	F	S
		1	2	3	4	5
6	7	8	9	10	11	12
13	14	15	16	17	18	19
20	21	22	23	24	25	26
27	28	29	30	31		

Waves of Grief

Down in the depths of your weary sorrow, God is there, calling to you, deep to deep. By day, as you work and try to think a clear path through the fog, He directs His love toward you, surrounding you with comfort. At night, God sings over you, like a mother singing a lullaby to her frightened child. God reminds you that you are never ever alone.

Goals *for* This Month

Deep calls to deep in the roar of your waterfalls;
all your waves and breakers have swept over me.

PSALM 42:7 NIV

September 2024

S	M	T	W	T	F	S
1	2	3	4	5	6	7
8	9	10	11	12	13	14
15	16	17	18	19	20	21
22	23	24	25	26	27	28
29	30					

When an adverse circumstance brings a shadow over your life, be brave and wise. Call on God. Ask for His help and light—and He will grant your request.

to-do list

- [ ] ....
- [ ] ....
- [ ] ....
- [ ] ....
- [ ] ....
- [ ] ....
- [ ] ....
- [ ] ....
- [ ] ....
- [ ] ....
- [ ] ....
- [ ] ....
- [ ] ....
- [ ] ....
- [ ] ....
- [ ] ....
- [ ] ....
- [ ] ....

SUNDAY, September 1

MONDAY, September 2   *Labor Day*

TUESDAY, September 3

WEDNESDAY, September 4

THURSDAY, September 5

FRIDAY, September 6

SATURDAY, September 7

☐ ....
☐ ....
☐ ....
☐ ....
☐ ....
☐ ....
☐ ....
☐ ....
☐ ....
☐ ....
☐ ....
☐ ....

Jabez was more honorable than his brothers. His mother named him Jabez and said, "I gave birth to him in pain." Jabez called out to the God of Israel: "If only You would bless me, extend my border, let Your hand be with me, and keep me from harm, so that I will not cause any pain." And God granted his request.
1 CHRONICLES 4:9–10 HCSB

September 2024

God doesn't expect us to always make right choices. After all, He made us. He is not surprised when we fail. So why hide? Come out, come out, wherever you are, and share your story. You'll be glad you did!

to-do list

- [ ]
- [ ]
- [ ]
- [ ]
- [ ]
- [ ]
- [ ]
- [ ]
- [ ]
- [ ]
- [ ]
- [ ]
- [ ]
- [ ]
- [ ]
- [ ]
- [ ]
- [ ]
- [ ]
- [ ]

SUNDAY, September 8

MONDAY, September 9

TUESDAY, September 10

WEDNESDAY, September 11

THURSDAY, September 12

FRIDAY, September 13

SATURDAY, September 14

to-do list

- [ ]
- [ ]
- [ ]
- [ ]
- [ ]
- [ ]
- [ ]
- [ ]
- [ ]
- [ ]
- [ ]
- [ ]
- [ ]
- [ ]
- [ ]
- [ ]
- [ ]
- [ ]
- [ ]
- [ ]

You are my hiding place; you protect me from trouble.
PSALM 32:7 CSB

September 2024

S	M	T	W	T	F	S
1	2	3	4	5	6	7
8	9	10	11	12	13	14
15	16	17	18	19	20	21
22	23	24	25	26	27	28
29	30					

God's promises to you may at times seem impossible of fulfillment, but God wants you to believe them. No matter how long it takes for Him to bring the miracle about, have faith that He will—in His time. And while you're waiting, keep praying. Keep believing. Keep expecting. And God will do the impossible in your life.

to-do list

☐ ....
☐ ....
☐ ....
☐ ....
☐ ....
☐ ....
☐ ....
☐ ....
☐ ....
☐ ....
☐ ....
☐ ....
☐ ....
☐ ....
☐ ....
☐ ....
☐ ....
☐ ....

SUNDAY, September 15

MONDAY, September 16

TUESDAY, September 17

WEDNESDAY, September 18

....
....
....
....
....

THURSDAY, September 19

....
....
....
....
....

FRIDAY, September 20

....
....
....
....
....

SATURDAY, September 21

....
....
....
....
....

to-do list

- [ ] ....
- [ ] ....
- [ ] ....
- [ ] ....
- [ ] ....
- [ ] ....
- [ ] ....
- [ ] ....
- [ ] ....
- [ ] ....
- [ ] ....
- [ ] ....
- [ ] ....
- [ ] ....

The angel said, "I am Gabriel, the sentinel of God, sent especially to bring you this glad news. But because you won't believe me, you'll be unable to say a word until the day of your son's birth. Every word I've spoken to you will come true on time—God's time."

LUKE 1:19–20 MSG

September 2024

S	M	T	W	T	F	S
1	2	3	4	5	6	7
8	9	10	11	12	13	14
15	16	17	18	19	20	21
22	23	24	25	26	27	28
29	30					

Choose the high road, the right way, no matter how enticing the temptation or shortcut that comes your way, for God is with you. And as you keep in step with Him, refusing to get sidelined by fear or temptation, God will make all you do successful.

to-do list

- ☐ ....
- ☐ ....
- ☐ ....
- ☐ ....
- ☐ ....
- ☐ ....
- ☐ ....
- ☐ ....
- ☐ ....
- ☐ ....
- ☐ ....
- ☐ ....
- ☐ ....
- ☐ ....
- ☐ ....
- ☐ ....
- ☐ ....
- ☐ ....

SUNDAY, September 22   *First Day of Autumn*

MONDAY, September 23

TUESDAY, September 24

WEDNESDAY, September 25

THURSDAY, September 26

FRIDAY, September 27

SATURDAY, September 28

- ☐
- ☐
- ☐
- ☐
- ☐
- ☐
- ☐
- ☐
- ☐
- ☐
- ☐
- ☐
- ☐
- ☐
- ☐

Joseph was well-built and handsome. After some time his master's wife looked longingly at Joseph and said, "Sleep with me." But he refused.... "How could I do such a great evil and sin against God?"

GENESIS 39:6–9 HCSB

October 2024

SUNDAY	MONDAY	TUESDAY	WEDNESDAY
29	30	1	2
6	7	8	9
13	14 *Columbus Day*	15	16
20	21	22	23
27	28	29	30

THURSDAY	FRIDAY	SATURDAY
3	4	5
10	11	12
17	18	19
24	25	26
31	1	2
Halloween		

SEPTEMBER

S	M	T	W	T	F	S
1	2	3	4	5	6	7
8	9	10	11	12	13	14
15	16	17	18	19	20	21
22	23	24	25	26	27	28
29	30					

NOVEMBER

S	M	T	W	T	F	S
					1	2
3	4	5	6	7	8	9
10	11	12	13	14	15	16
17	18	19	20	21	22	23
24	25	26	27	28	29	30

In the Details

Use your head *and* your heart. Be discerning. Hang on to the truth instead of letting yourself drown in the details. Don't miss out on what God has for you simply because you believe you know exactly how and what God is going to give. Be open to the mystery of the living and breathing Lord of all.

Goals *for* This Month

*"Don't be hypercritical; use your head—and heart!—
to discern what is right, to test what is authentically right."*
JOHN 7:24 MSG

September-October 2024

S	M	T	W	T	F	S
		1	2	3	4	5
6	7	8	9	10	11	12
13	14	15	16	17	18	19
20	21	22	23	24	25	26
27	28	29	30	31		

Your prayers can provide all the strength, courage, and hope you need to follow God's leading. Whether lengthy prayers or short arrow prayers, your request to God should be shared to help inspire others. Doing so sets off a chain of encouragement.

to-do list

- [ ]
- [ ]
- [ ]
- [ ]
- [ ]
- [ ]
- [ ]
- [ ]
- [ ]
- [ ]
- [ ]
- [ ]
- [ ]
- [ ]
- [ ]
- [ ]
- [ ]
- [ ]
- [ ]

SUNDAY, September 29

MONDAY, September 30

TUESDAY, October 1

WEDNESDAY, October 2

....

....

....

....

....

THURSDAY, October 3

....

....

....

....

....

FRIDAY, October 4

....

....

....

....

....

SATURDAY, October 5

....

....

....

....

....

to-do list

☐ ....
☐ ....
☐ ....
☐ ....
☐ ....
☐ ....
☐ ....
☐ ....
☐ ....
☐ ....
☐ ....
☐ ....
☐ ....

*I was very much afraid.
I said to the king, "Let
the king live forever.
Why should my face not
be sad when the city,
the place of my fathers'
graves, lies waste and
its gates destroyed by
fire?" Then the king said
to me, "What are you
asking for?" So I prayed
to the God of heaven.*
NEHEMIAH 2:2–4 NLV

October 2024

S	M	T	W	T	F	S
		1	2	3	4	5
6	7	8	9	10	11	12
13	14	15	16	17	18	19
20	21	22	23	24	25	26
27	28	29	30	31		

God is calling us out of our comfort zone and into a new place, a new life. God wants us to have faith in Him and courageously say, "I will go," knowing that as we do so, we're not only following God but also may be answering someone else's prayer.

to-do list

- ☐ ....
- ☐ ....
- ☐ ....
- ☐ ....
- ☐ ....
- ☐ ....
- ☐ ....
- ☐ ....
- ☐ ....
- ☐ ....
- ☐ ....
- ☐ ....
- ☐ ....
- ☐ ....
- ☐ ....
- ☐ ....
- ☐ ....
- ☐ ....

SUNDAY, October 6

MONDAY, October 7

TUESDAY, October 8

WEDNESDAY, October 9

....
....
....
....
....

THURSDAY, October 10

....
....
....
....
....

FRIDAY, October 11

....
....
....
....
....

SATURDAY, October 12

....
....
....
....
....

"This is from the LORD; we have no choice in the matter.... Take [Rebekah] and go, and let her be a wife for your master's son."... So they said, "Let's call the girl and ask her opinion." They called Rebekah and said to her, "Will you go with this man?" She replied, "I will go."
GENESIS 24:50–51, 57–58 HCSB

October 2024

S	M	T	W	T	F	S
		1	2	3	4	5
6	7	8	9	10	11	12
13	14	15	16	17	18	19
20	21	22	23	24	25	26
27	28	29	30	31		

God has called each of us to live out His purpose for us. Perhaps this is your moment, your reminder, to pray for the courage you'll need for such a time as this.

to-do list

- [ ]
- [ ]
- [ ]
- [ ]
- [ ]
- [ ]
- [ ]
- [ ]
- [ ]
- [ ]
- [ ]
- [ ]
- [ ]
- [ ]
- [ ]
- [ ]
- [ ]
- [ ]
- [ ]

SUNDAY, October 13

MONDAY, October 14   *Columbus Day*

TUESDAY, October 15

WEDNESDAY, October 16

....
....
....
....
....

THURSDAY, October 17

....
....
....
....
....

FRIDAY, October 18

....
....
....
....
....

SATURDAY, October 19

....
....
....
....
....

to-do list

☐ ....
☐ ....
☐ ....
☐ ....
☐ ....
☐ ....
☐ ....
☐ ....
☐ ....
☐ ....
☐ ....
☐ ....
☐ ....
☐ ....
☐ ....
☐ ....

*"Who knows, perhaps
you have come to
your royal position for
such a time as this."*
ESTHER 4:14 HCSB

October 2024

S	M	T	W	T	F	S
		1	2	3	4	5
6	7	8	9	10	11	12
13	14	15	16	17	18	19
20	21	22	23	24	25	26
27	28	29	30	31		

To be strong, even in times of trouble, we have to practice being strong. We have to discipline ourselves to seek truth every day. At first our strength—and our faith—may be small, but with practice and discipline, it can grow into something that can stand up under enormous amounts of pressure.

to-do list

- [ ] ....
- [ ] ....
- [ ] ....
- [ ] ....
- [ ] ....
- [ ] ....
- [ ] ....
- [ ] ....
- [ ] ....
- [ ] ....
- [ ] ....
- [ ] ....
- [ ] ....
- [ ] ....
- [ ] ....
- [ ] ....
- [ ] ....
- [ ] ....
- [ ] ....

SUNDAY, October 20

MONDAY, October 21

TUESDAY, October 22

WEDNESDAY, October 23

....

....

....

....

....

THURSDAY, October 24

....

....

....

....

....

FRIDAY, October 25

....

....

....

....

....

SATURDAY, October 26

....

....

....

....

....

- ☐ ....
- ☐ ....
- ☐ ....
- ☐ ....
- ☐ ....
- ☐ ....
- ☐ ....
- ☐ ....
- ☐ ....
- ☐ ....
- ☐ ....
- ☐ ....
- ☐ ....
- ☐ ....
- ☐ ....
- ☐ ....
- ☐ ....
- ☐ ....

*If you falter in a time
of trouble, how small
is your strength!*
PROVERBS 24:10 NIV

November 2024

SUNDAY	MONDAY	TUESDAY	WEDNESDAY
27	28	29	30
3 *Daylight Saving Time Ends*	4	5 *Election Day*	6
10	11 *Veterans Day*	12	13
17	18	19	20
24	25	26	27

THURSDAY	FRIDAY	SATURDAY
31	1	2
7	8	9
14	15	16
21	22	23
28	29	30
Thanksgiving Day		

....
....
....
....
....
....
....
....
....
....
....
....
....

OCTOBER

S	M	T	W	T	F	S
		1	2	3	4	5
6	7	8	9	10	11	12
13	14	15	16	17	18	19
20	21	22	23	24	25	26
27	28	29	30	31		

DECEMBER

S	M	T	W	T	F	S
1	2	3	4	5	6	7
8	9	10	11	12	13	14
15	16	17	18	19	20	21
22	23	24	25	26	27	28
29	30	31				

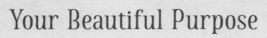

Your Beautiful Purpose

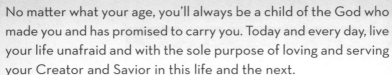

No matter what your age, you'll always be a child of the God who made you and has promised to carry you. Today and every day, live your life unafraid and with the sole purpose of loving and serving your Creator and Savior in this life and the next.

Goals *for* This Month

Even to your old age I am He, and even to
hair white with age will I carry you. I have made,
and I will bear; yes, I will carry and will save you.
ISAIAH 46:4 AMPC

October-November 2024

S	M	T	W	T	F	S
					1	2
3	4	5	6	7	8	9
10	11	12	13	14	15	16
17	18	19	20	21	22	23
24	25	26	27	28	29	30

When you take time to snuggle up to Jesus, to become more intimate with Him, telling Him all your desires, you'll become stronger, feel more worthy, just by being with Him. Your fears will fade as your faith blooms. . .in Him.

to-do list

- ☐ ....
- ☐ ....
- ☐ ....
- ☐ ....
- ☐ ....
- ☐ ....
- ☐ ....
- ☐ ....
- ☐ ....
- ☐ ....
- ☐ ....
- ☐ ....
- ☐ ....
- ☐ ....
- ☐ ....
- ☐ ....
- ☐ ....
- ☐ ....
- ☐ ....

SUNDAY, October 27

MONDAY, October 28

TUESDAY, October 29

WEDNESDAY, October 30

THURSDAY, October 31   *Halloween*

FRIDAY, November 1

SATURDAY, November 2

to-do list

- [ ]
- [ ]
- [ ]
- [ ]
- [ ]
- [ ]
- [ ]
- [ ]
- [ ]
- [ ]
- [ ]
- [ ]
- [ ]
- [ ]
- [ ]
- [ ]
- [ ]

*My beloved
[shepherd]. . . [I can
feel] his left hand under
my head and his right
hand embraces me!*
SONG OF SOLOMON 2:3, 6
AMPC

November 2024

S	M	T	W	T	F	S
					1	2
3	4	5	6	7	8	9
10	11	12	13	14	15	16
17	18	19	20	21	22	23
24	25	26	27	28	29	30

When you're in the wilderness, out of resources, including courage, look to God. He hears your cries. He'll give you everything you need to continue. And He won't just refill your drinking bottle; He will open your eyes to a well of abundant waters.

to-do list

- [ ] ....
- [ ] ....
- [ ] ....
- [ ] ....
- [ ] ....
- [ ] ....
- [ ] ....
- [ ] ....
- [ ] ....
- [ ] ....
- [ ] ....
- [ ] ....
- [ ] ....
- [ ] ....
- [ ] ....
- [ ] ....
- [ ] ....
- [ ] ....

SUNDAY, November 3　　　*Daylight Saving Time Ends*

MONDAY, November 4

TUESDAY, November 5　　　*Election Day*

WEDNESDAY, November 6

THURSDAY, November 7

FRIDAY, November 8

SATURDAY, November 9

- [ ] ....
- [ ] ....
- [ ] ....
- [ ] ....
- [ ] ....
- [ ] ....
- [ ] ....
- [ ] ....
- [ ] ....
- [ ] ....
- [ ] ....
- [ ] ....
- [ ] ....

*"What's wrong, Hagar?
Don't be afraid. God has
heard the boy and knows
the fix he's in. Up now;
go get the boy. Hold him
tight. I'm going to make
of him a great nation."
Just then God opened
her eyes. She looked.
She saw a well of water.*
GENESIS 21:17–19 MSG

November 2024

S	M	T	W	T	F	S
					1	2
3	4	5	6	7	8	9
10	11	12	13	14	15	16
17	18	19	20	21	22	23
24	25	26	27	28	29	30

Whenever you're challenged or in distress, remember that you too can trust God's promise: "I will be with you when you pass through the waters, and when you pass through the rivers, they will not overwhelm you. You will not be scorched when you walk through the fire, and the flame will not burn you" (Isaiah 43:2 HCSB).

to-do list

- [ ]
- [ ]
- [ ]
- [ ]
- [ ]
- [ ]
- [ ]
- [ ]
- [ ]
- [ ]
- [ ]
- [ ]
- [ ]
- [ ]
- [ ]
- [ ]
- [ ]
- [ ]

SUNDAY, November 10

MONDAY, November 11   *Veterans Day*

TUESDAY, November 12

WEDNESDAY, November 13

THURSDAY, November 14

FRIDAY, November 15

SATURDAY, November 16

- [ ]
- [ ]
- [ ]
- [ ]
- [ ]
- [ ]
- [ ]
- [ ]
- [ ]
- [ ]
- [ ]
- [ ]
- [ ]

"The God we serve can rescue us from your roaring furnace and anything else you might cook up, O king. But even if he doesn't, it wouldn't make a bit of difference, O king. We still wouldn't serve your gods or worship the gold statue you set up."

DANIEL 3:17–18 MSG

November 2024

S	M	T	W	T	F	S
					1	2
3	4	5	6	7	8	9
10	11	12	13	14	15	16
17	18	19	20	21	22	23
24	25	26	27	28	29	30

God is the reason we are where we are. God is the reason that any good thing has happened to us at all. If we give in to temptation and commit acts of sin, then we are not just doing bad things to others or ourselves but also sinning against God.

to-do list

- [ ] ....
- [ ] ....
- [ ] ....
- [ ] ....
- [ ] ....
- [ ] ....
- [ ] ....
- [ ] ....
- [ ] ....
- [ ] ....
- [ ] ....
- [ ] ....
- [ ] ....
- [ ] ....
- [ ] ....
- [ ] ....
- [ ] ....
- [ ] ....

SUNDAY, November 17

MONDAY, November 18

TUESDAY, November 19

WEDNESDAY, November 20

to-do list

THURSDAY, November 21

FRIDAY, November 22

SATURDAY, November 23

"How then could I do such a wicked thing and sin against God?"
GENESIS 39:9 NIV

November 2024

S	M	T	W	T	F	S
					1	2
3	4	5	6	7	8	9
10	11	12	13	14	15	16
17	18	19	20	21	22	23
24	25	26	27	28	29	30

Stop tiptoeing around what-ifs and maybes. Get in there, immerse yourself in God's promises, and then come up in the power of Christ, ready, willing, and able to wait, watch, and expect God to make good on His Word. And you'll be right with God.

to-do list

- [ ]
- [ ]
- [ ]
- [ ]
- [ ]
- [ ]
- [ ]
- [ ]
- [ ]
- [ ]
- [ ]
- [ ]
- [ ]
- [ ]
- [ ]
- [ ]
- [ ]
- [ ]

SUNDAY, November 24

MONDAY, November 25

TUESDAY, November 26

WEDNESDAY, November 27

- [ ] ....
- [ ] ....
- [ ] ....
- [ ] ....
- [ ] ....
- [ ] ....
- [ ] ....

THURSDAY, November 28   *Thanksgiving Day*

- [ ] ....
- [ ] ....
- [ ] ....
- [ ] ....
- [ ] ....
- [ ] ....

FRIDAY, November 29

- [ ] ....
- [ ] ....
- [ ] ....

[Abraham] didn't tiptoe around God's promise asking cautiously skeptical questions. He plunged into the promise and came up strong, ready for God, sure that God would make good on what he had said.
ROMANS 4:20–21 MSG

SATURDAY, November 30

December 2024

SUNDAY	MONDAY	TUESDAY	WEDNESDAY
1	2	3	4
8	9	10	11
15	16	17	18
22	23	24 *Christmas Eve*	25 *Hanukkah Begins at Sundown* *Christmas Day*
29	30	31 *New Year's Eve*	1

THURSDAY	FRIDAY	SATURDAY
5	6	7
12	13	14
19	20	21 *First Day of Winter*
26	27	28
2	3	4

notes

....
....
....
....
....
....
....
....
....
....
....
....
....

NOVEMBER

S	M	T	W	T	F	S
					1	2
3	4	5	6	7	8	9
10	11	12	13	14	15	16
17	18	19	20	21	22	23
24	25	26	27	28	29	30

JANUARY

S	M	T	W	T	F	S
			1	2	3	4
5	6	7	8	9	10	11
12	13	14	15	16	17	18
19	20	21	22	23	24	25
26	27	28	29	30	31	

Where You Are with God

When you worry about the things of this life, you take your eyes off God. You worry because on some level you think you can figure out all the answers—you can supply your own needs. But God wants you to depend on Him. He wants you to lean on Him. It's just not about you. And it's not about just you. It's about where you are with God.

Goals *for* This Month

"But when you give to the needy, do not let your left hand know
what your right hand is doing, so that your giving may be in secret.
Then your Father, who sees what is done in secret, will reward you."

MATTHEW 6:3-4 NIV

December 2024

S	M	T	W	T	F	S
1	2	3	4	5	6	7
8	9	10	11	12	13	14
15	16	17	18	19	20	21
22	23	24	25	26	27	28
29	30	31				

Your treasures in heaven are much more valuable than those on earth. The best thing you can do for yourself, your family, and God is to be courageous enough to forget about your life and focus on Jesus. In doing so, you'll gain both.

to-do list

- [ ] ....
- [ ] ....
- [ ] ....
- [ ] ....
- [ ] ....
- [ ] ....
- [ ] ....
- [ ] ....
- [ ] ....
- [ ] ....
- [ ] ....
- [ ] ....
- [ ] ....
- [ ] ....
- [ ] ....
- [ ] ....
- [ ] ....
- [ ] ....

SUNDAY, December 1

MONDAY, December 2

TUESDAY, December 3

WEDNESDAY, December 4

THURSDAY, December 5

FRIDAY, December 6

SATURDAY, December 7

to-do list

- [ ]
- [ ]
- [ ]
- [ ]
- [ ]
- [ ]
- [ ]
- [ ]
- [ ]
- [ ]
- [ ]
- [ ]
- [ ]

"If you don't go all the way with me, through thick and thin, you don't deserve me. If your first concern is to look after yourself, you'll never find yourself. But if you forget about yourself and look to me, you'll find both yourself and me."
MATTHEW 10:39 MSG

December 2024

S	M	T	W	T	F	S
1	2	3	4	5	6	7
8	9	10	11	12	13	14
15	16	17	18	19	20	21
22	23	24	25	26	27	28
29	30	31				

We sometimes don't even know what we ought to pray for—that's how clueless we are. But God knows. The Spirit prays for us—taking what's in our hearts and minds and weaving it together into a wordless whisper of longing and hope to God.

to-do list

- [ ]
- [ ]
- [ ]
- [ ]
- [ ]
- [ ]
- [ ]
- [ ]
- [ ]
- [ ]
- [ ]
- [ ]
- [ ]
- [ ]
- [ ]
- [ ]
- [ ]
- [ ]

SUNDAY, December 8

MONDAY, December 9

TUESDAY, December 10

WEDNESDAY, December 11

THURSDAY, December 12

FRIDAY, December 13

SATURDAY, December 14

- [ ]
- [ ]
- [ ]
- [ ]
- [ ]
- [ ]
- [ ]
- [ ]
- [ ]
- [ ]
- [ ]
- [ ]
- [ ]
- [ ]
- [ ]
- [ ]
- [ ]

And we know that in all things God works for the good of those who love him, who have been called according to his purpose.
ROMANS 8:28 NIV

December 2024

S	M	T	W	T	F	S
1	2	3	4	5	6	7
8	9	10	11	12	13	14
15	16	17	18	19	20	21
22	23	24	25	26	27	28
29	30	31				

Whenever you come across what sounds like an impossible promise of God's, take another look. See it using eyes of faith. Remember that God is the doer of the impossible. Nothing in heaven or on earth is beyond His means. He can work a miracle for you.

to-do list

☐ ....
☐ ....
☐ ....
☐ ....
☐ ....
☐ ....
☐ ....
☐ ....
☐ ....
☐ ....
☐ ....
☐ ....
☐ ....
☐ ....
☐ ....
☐ ....
☐ ....
☐ ....
☐ ....

SUNDAY, December 15

MONDAY, December 16

TUESDAY, December 17

WEDNESDAY, December 18

....
....
....
....
....
....

THURSDAY, December 19

....
....
....
....
....

FRIDAY, December 20

....
....
....
....
....

SATURDAY, December 21   *First Day of Winter*

....
....
....
....
....

- ☐ ....
- ☐ ....
- ☐ ....
- ☐ ....
- ☐ ....
- ☐ ....
- ☐ ....
- ☐ ....
- ☐ ....
- ☐ ....
- ☐ ....
- ☐ ....
- ☐ ....
- ☐ ....
- ☐ ....
- ☐ ....
- ☐ ....
- ☐ ....
- ☐ ....

*"Is anything too
hard for GOD?"*
GENESIS 18:14 MSG

December 2024

S	M	T	W	T	F	S
1	2	3	4	5	6	7
8	9	10	11	12	13	14
15	16	17	18	19	20	21
22	23	24	25	26	27	28
29	30	31				

The God who has "great power and mighty strength" (Isaiah 40:26 NIV) does not let any one of us go missing—He knows us each by name and calls us to Him. Like a strong shepherd, our God scoops us up when we are far away from Him and holds us tightly to His heart. He whispers to us to stay close and not stray too far. And then He lets us go again.

to-do list

☐ ....
☐ ....
☐ ....
☐ ....
☐ ....
☐ ....
☐ ....
☐ ....
☐ ....
☐ ....
☐ ....
☐ ....
☐ ....
☐ ....
☐ ....
☐ ....
☐ ....
☐ ....
☐ ....

SUNDAY, December 22

MONDAY, December 23

TUESDAY, December 24   *Christmas Eve*

WEDNESDAY, December 25   *Christmas Day*
                               Hanukkah Begins at Sundown

....

....

....

....

THURSDAY, December 26

....

....

....

....

....

FRIDAY, December 27

....

....

....

....

....

SATURDAY, December 28

....

....

....

....

....

to-do list

☐ ....
☐ ....
☐ ....
☐ ....
☐ ....
☐ ....
☐ ....
☐ ....
☐ ....
☐ ....
☐ ....
☐ ....
☐ ....
☐ ....
☐ ....
☐ ....
☐ ....
☐ ....
☐ ....
☐ ....

*He gathers the lambs
in his arms and carries
them close to his heart.*
ISAIAH 40:11 NIV

December 2024–January 2025

S	M	T	W	T	F	S
1	2	3	4	5	6	7
8	9	10	11	12	13	14
15	16	17	18	19	20	21
22	23	24	25	26	27	28
29	30	31				

God has a perfect timetable. His job is to work it out. Yours is to be patient while He does so, steering clear of fear as you stay on the faithful course.

to-do list

- [ ] ....
- [ ] ....
- [ ] ....
- [ ] ....
- [ ] ....
- [ ] ....
- [ ] ....
- [ ] ....
- [ ] ....
- [ ] ....
- [ ] ....
- [ ] ....
- [ ] ....
- [ ] ....
- [ ] ....
- [ ] ....
- [ ] ....
- [ ] ....

SUNDAY, December 29

MONDAY, December 30

TUESDAY, December 31   *New Year's Eve*

WEDNESDAY, January 1

New Year's Day

....

....

....

....

....

THURSDAY, January 2

....

....

....

....

....

FRIDAY, January 3

....

....

....

....

....

SATURDAY, January 4

....

....

....

....

....

to-do list

- ☐ ....
- ☐ ....
- ☐ ....
- ☐ ....
- ☐ ....
- ☐ ....
- ☐ ....
- ☐ ....
- ☐ ....
- ☐ ....
- ☐ ....
- ☐ ....
- ☐ ....
- ☐ ....
- ☐ ....
- ☐ ....
- ☐ ....
- ☐ ....

Be like those who stay the course with committed faith and then get everything promised to them.
HEBREWS 6:12 MSG

CONTACTS

Name:

Address:

Phone: Mobile:

Email:

Name:

Address:

Phone: Mobile:

Email:

Name:

Address:

Phone: Mobile:

Email:

Name:

Address:

Phone: Mobile:

Email:

CONTACTS

Name:

Address:

Phone: Mobile:

Email:

Name:

Address:

Phone: Mobile:

Email:

Name:

Address:

Phone: Mobile:

Email:

Name:

Address:

Phone: Mobile:

Email:

CONTACTS

Name:

Address:

Phone: Mobile:

Email:

Name:

Address:

Phone: Mobile:

Email:

Name:

Address:

Phone: Mobile:

Email:

Name:

Address:

Phone: Mobile:

Email:

CONTACTS

Name:

Address:

Phone: Mobile:

Email:

Name:

Address:

Phone: Mobile:

Email:

Name:

Address:

Phone: Mobile:

Email:

Name:

Address:

Phone: Mobile:

Email:

CONTACTS

Name:

Address:

Phone: Mobile:

Email:

Name:

Address:

Phone: Mobile:

Email:

Name:

Address:

Phone: Mobile:

Email:

Name:

Address:

Phone: Mobile:

Email:

CONTACTS

Name:

Address:

Phone: Mobile:

Email:

Name:

Address:

Phone: Mobile:

Email:

Name:

Address:

Phone: Mobile:

Email:

Name:

Address:

Phone: Mobile:

Email:

CONTACTS

Name:

Address:

Phone: Mobile:

Email:

Name:

Address:

Phone: Mobile:

Email:

Name:

Address:

Phone: Mobile:

Email:

Name:

Address:

Phone: Mobile:

Email:

CONTACTS

Name:

Address:

Phone: Mobile:

Email:

Name:

Address:

Phone: Mobile:

Email:

Name:

Address:

Phone: Mobile:

Email:

Name:

Address:

Phone: Mobile:

Email:

CONTACTS

Name:

Address:

Phone: Mobile:

Email:

Name:

Address:

Phone: Mobile:

Email:

Name:

Address:

Phone: Mobile:

Email:

Name:

Address:

Phone: Mobile:

Email:

CONTACTS

Name:

Address:

Phone: Mobile:

Email:

Name:

Address:

Phone: Mobile:

Email:

Name:

Address:

Phone: Mobile:

Email:

Name:

Address:

Phone: Mobile:

Email:

CONTACTS

Name:

Address:

Phone: Mobile:

Email:

Name:

Address:

Phone: Mobile:

Email:

Name:

Address:

Phone: Mobile:

Email:

Name:

Address:

Phone: Mobile:

Email: